Opa: Up and Running

Henri Binsztok, Adam Koprowski, and Ida Swarczewskaja

Beijing · Cambridge · Farnham · Köln · Sebastopol · Tokyo

Opa: Up and Running

by Henri Binsztok, Adam Koprowski, and Ida Swarczewskaja

Copyright © 2013 MLstate. All rights reserved.

Printed in the United States of America.

Published by O'Reilly Media, Inc., 1005 Gravenstein Highway North, Sebastopol, CA 95472.

O'Reilly books may be purchased for educational, business, or sales promotional use. Online editions are also available for most titles (*http://my.safaribooksonline.com*). For more information, contact our corporate/institutional sales department: 800-998-9938 or *corporate@oreilly.com*.

Editors: Simon St. Laurent and Meghan Blanchette
Production Editor: Rachel Steely

Copyeditor: Audrey Doyle
Proofreader: Rachel Steely
Cover Designer: Karen Montgomery
Interior Designer: David Futato
Illustrator: Rebecca Demarest

February 2013:   First Edition

Revision History for the First Edition:

2013-02-20   First release

See *http://oreilly.com/catalog/errata.csp?isbn=9781449328856* for release details.

ISBN: 978-1-449-32885-6

[LSI]

Table of Contents

Preface

Modern web applications represent the new way to write software. Facebook, Twitter, and Wikipedia are some well-known examples of such applications. They run on servers, and users can access them with a browser via either desktop or mobile devices. We refer to these as "modern" applications because they combine a rich user interface with real-time interaction and the capability to connect with online services, among other capabilities.

Opa is a programming framework for JavaScript that enables you to easily write modern web applications that have all the aforementioned cool features. This book is a gentle introduction to Opa.

What Is Opa?

Traditionally, many different technologies and languages are involved when writing web applications. Not so with Opa! Opa is the only technology you need to know to write the code that runs on the client (in the browser) and the code that runs on the server, including database queries.

Opa natively supports the web platform, which is a set of technologies that includes HTML5 and CSS, and it automates many aspects of modern web application programming: Ajax/Comet client/server communication, event-driven and nonblocking code transformations, etc.

One of the main distinctive features of Opa is strong static typing, with type inference. This means that every application you write is checked by a program called a typechecker that automatically tracks inconsistencies in the application. Typing enables Opa programmers to debug applications quickly, and increases application safety and security.

As a final step, Opa generates standard code: JavaScript for the client side, Node.js, and MongoDB for the server side.

The philosophy of Opa is to support multiple platforms. It is possible to extend Opa to support different backends.

How Do I Work with Opa?

Working with Opa is as easy as 1, 2, 3:

1. Write your application code in a text editor.
2. Generate your application by invoking Opa.
3. Run and/or deploy your application online.

In "Installing Opa" (page 3), you will learn how to install Opa and create your first application. Then you will develop two real applications with Opa: a mini-Wikipedia and a mini-Twitter.

The applications you develop with Opa are standard JavaScript projects that run both in the browser (where JavaScript is by far the most prevalent) and on the server. On the server side (also called the backend), the applications rely on two popular technologies for the runtime:

- Node.js, which allows you to execute JavaScript code on the server
- MongoDB, which is a NoSQL database server

Both technologies were chosen for their ability to *scale*, that is, easily add servers to handle more clients when your application becomes hugely popular.

Conventions Used in This Book

The following typographical conventions are used in this book:

Italic
> Indicates new terms, URLs, email addresses, filenames, and file extensions

`Constant width`
> Used for program listings, as well as within paragraphs to refer to program elements such as variable or function names, databases, data types, environment variables, statements, and keywords

`Constant width bold`
> Shows commands or other text that should be typed literally by the user

`Constant width italic`
> Shows text that should be replaced with user-supplied values or by values determined by context

This icon signifies a tip, suggestion, or general note.

 This icon indicates a warning or caution.

Using Code Examples

This book is here to help you get your job done. In general, if this book includes code examples, you may use the code in this book in your programs and documentation. You do not need to contact us for permission unless you're reproducing a significant portion of the code. For example, writing a program that uses several chunks of code from this book does not require permission. Selling or distributing a CD-ROM of examples from O'Reilly books does require permission. Answering a question by citing this book and quoting example code does not require permission. Incorporating a significant amount of example code from this book into your product's documentation does require permission.

We appreciate, but do not require, attribution. An attribution usually includes the title, author, publisher, and ISBN. For example: "*Opa: Up and Running* by Henri Binsztok, Adam Koprowski, and Ida Swarczewskaja (O'Reilly). Copyright 2013 MLstate, 978-1-449-32885-6."

If you feel your use of code examples falls outside fair use or the permission given here, feel free to contact us at *permissions@oreilly.com*.

Safari® Books Online

 *Safari Books Online* is an on-demand digital library that delivers expert content in both book and video form from the world's leading authors in technology and business.

Technology professionals, software developers, web designers, and business and creative professionals use Safari Books Online as their primary resource for research, problem solving, learning, and certification training.

Safari Books Online offers a range of product mixes and pricing programs for organizations, government agencies, and individuals. Subscribers have access to thousands of books, training videos, and prepublication manuscripts in one fully searchable database from publishers like O'Reilly Media, Prentice Hall Professional, Addison-Wesley Professional, Microsoft Press, Sams, Que, Peachpit Press, Focal Press, Cisco Press, John Wiley & Sons, Syngress, Morgan Kaufmann, IBM Redbooks, Packt, Adobe Press, FT

Press, Apress, Manning, New Riders, McGraw-Hill, Jones & Bartlett, Course Technology, and dozens more. For more information about Safari Books Online, please visit us online.

How to Contact Us

Please address comments and questions concerning this book to the publisher:

O'Reilly Media, Inc.
1005 Gravenstein Highway North
Sebastopol, CA 95472
800-998-9938 (in the United States or Canada)
707-829-0515 (international or local)
707-829-0104 (fax)

We have a web page for this book, where we list errata, examples, and any additional information. You can access this page at *http://oreil.ly/Opa_1E*.

To comment or ask technical questions about this book, send email to *bookques tions@oreilly.com*.

For more information about our books, courses, conferences, and news, see our website at *http://www.oreilly.com*.

Find us on Facebook: *http://facebook.com/oreilly*

Follow us on Twitter: *http://twitter.com/oreillymedia*

Watch us on YouTube: *http://www.youtube.com/oreillymedia*

Acknowledgments

The authors would like to thank Alok Menghrajani, who did a thorough review of the original draft of the book. Opa would never exist without the work of its contributors, including the core developers of Opa: Cédric Soulas, Frédéric Ye, Norman Scaife, and Quentin Bourgerie. Thank you for your impressive work.

PART I

Coding a Mini Wikipedia

This book is organized into two parts. In this first part, we start from the beginning and progress to coding a wiki application that could later grow to match the features and scalability of Wikipedia.

The goal is ambitious, but Opa lowers the requirement. So let's jump in right now.

First Steps: Getting to Know Opa

In this chapter, you will get your first glimpse of Opa. You will learn how to install it, write an Opa program, and become familiar with the crucial steps in the development cycle.

Installing Opa

To install Opa, get the package for your architecture from Opa's website (*http://opalang.org*). At the time of this writing, installers are available for all major platforms: Mac OS X, Windows, Linux (generic, Ubuntu, and Fedora), and FreeBSD. These installers work with 64-bit architectures and, on some platforms, with 32-bit architectures.

On Mac OS X, you need to have Apple's Xcode command-line tools installed as well.

As an option, you can compile Opa from source, but we strongly recommend using packages to begin with.

Once you have downloaded Opa, you can that check it's correctly installed by opening a terminal and running the following:

```
Tokyo:~ henri$ opa --version
Opa compiler (c) MLstate -- version 1.0.7 -- build 4040
```

This gives you the Opa version and build number. Opa then checks that its runtime dependencies are also installed in your system and should guide you to install them if necessary. You are all set!

Installing Node.js

Opa uses Node.js to execute JavaScript code on the server. To install Node.js, get the package for your platform from the Node.js website (*http://nodejs.org*). Then type the following command in your terminal:

```
Tokyo:~ henri$ npm install -g ursa formidable
```

The -g stands for global and means that the node modules will be installed wherever
the Node.js program could easily find them.

Auto-Installing MongoDB

MongoDB is automatically installed and launched while you are running the Opa
application on the server.

 You can find up-to-date installation instructions online at *https://
github.com/MLstate/opalang/wiki/Getting-started.*

Our First Program

In this section, you will write and then run your first program. You'll then learn what
the code actually means, how to build the application, and what happens behind the
scenes.

Writing and Running the Code

You will write your Opa application code in a text editor. Any basic editor works, but
we recommend using one of the editors for which Opa-specific plug-ins exist, including:

- Sublime Text2 (*http://www.sublimetext.com/2*)
- Emacs (*http://www.gnu.org/software/emacs/*)
- Vim (*http://www.vim.org/*)
- Eclipse (*http://www.eclipse.org/*)

Please check the online Opa documentation (*https://github.com/MLstate/opalang/wiki/
Getting-started#wiki-ide*) for up-to-date information on how to set up your preferred
text editor.

Now open your editor and create a file that is named *hello.opa* and that contains the
following content:

```
Server.start(Server.http,
  { title: "Hello, world",
    page: function() { <h1>Hello, world</h1> }
  }
)
```

This is a very simple application that just displays a static Hello, world message. You
can run the application by typing the following command in a terminal:

```
Tokyo:~ henri$ opa hello.opa --
Http serving on http://localhost:8080
```

We will come back to this code later to discuss what actually happens here. For now, just point your browser to *http://localhost:8080* and you should see something similar to Figure 1-1.

Figure 1-1. Our first Opa program in action

What localhost:8080 Means

Usually, you open addresses in your browser that look like this: *facebook.com*. This so-called URL (Uniform Resource Locator) allows to locate Internet resources, similar to how you use street addresses you to locate buildings.

Referring to the URL used in the preceding code, *localhost* is the standard way to address the local machine, that is, *this* computer. The corresponding IP address, usually 127.0.0.1 or the name of your computer, will work as well.

The *8080* after the colon in the address is the *port* number. Domain names are used to locate sites; ports are used to distinguish different *services* within sites. If we were to compare URLs to street addresses, domain names would correspond to the country, city, and street, whereas the port would correspond to the house/apartment number.

The default port for web services is 80. However, running applications on port numbers smaller than 1024 often requires administrator rights; therefore, Opa chooses 8080 as the default port for its applications. You can change this with the `--port X` switch of the executable; for example:

```
Tokyo:~ henri$ ./hello.js --port 2012
```

Lastly, a URL may also contain a *path*, as in *http://example.com/this/andthat.html*, in which the path is */this/andthat.html*. The domain name and the path are handled separately. The domain name is used to locate the box running the service. To do this, browsers make requests on DNS servers that translate the name into the IP address of the service. When scaling, the DNS is the first technology to distribute the requests of many clients to different boxes. The path is used to locate a resource on the service. Originally, the path was used to locate a file on the service—perhaps a static resource such as an image or a script. But with modern frameworks such as Opa, most resources are virtual.

What the Code Means

Let's decipher the meaning of the four lines of code we wrote:

```
Server.start(Server.http,
  { title: "Hello, world",
    page: function() { <h1>Hello, world</h1> }
  }
)
```

`Server.start` is an entry point for Opa programs, much like `main` in Java or C, which launches the application web service. It takes two arguments: the server configuration and the definition of how the server should handle incoming requests. This second parameter can exist in many different forms, and you will learn more about them in Chapter 3.

Here we are using a variant that creates a simple application with a single page (which will be shown regardless of the URL). This variant is defined by a *record* with two fields: `title` and `page`, denoting the page title and content, respectively. If you are familiar with JavaScript, you will notice that Opa borrows the same `{ field1: val1, ... fieldN: valN }` syntax to denote records. You will learn more about records in "Records" (page 17).

The `title` field is a `string`, whereas `page` is a *function* that takes no arguments and returns the (X)HTML content of the page.

 HTML stands for *HyperText Markup Language* and is the standard markup language for web pages. If you are not familiar with it, we suggest that you grab a good book or some of the multitude of online resources on HTML.

HTML is a first-class citizen in Opa: it is a predefined data type with special support that allows it to be entered using its usual syntax. Opa supports the shiny and new HTML5 version of HTML. You will learn more about HTML5 features in Chapter 5.

What Happens When We Run Your Application

When you run your application by invoking `opa hello.opa --`, you actually perform two different operations:

1. You transform (or compile) the source code you have written into a runnable application.
2. You launch the runtime environment and execute your application.

Let's take a closer look at step 1. Opa is a JavaScript framework consisting of two pieces: a library and a compiler. The library is an approximate version of the prebuilt code you use in your applications, while the compiler is a strange and complex beast that performs several operations:

1. The compiler reads the Opa code you have written (that step is called *parsing*) and checks that the code is syntactically correct. For instance, if you forget a closing parenthesis in your code, you will get a parsing error.
2. If parsing succeeds, the compiler verifies more deeply that your application does not do silly things, by checking the consistency of the whole application. This major step is called *typechecking* and you will learn about it in detail in Chapter 2.
3. If typing succeeds, the compiler identifies which parts of the application run on the server, on the database, and on the client. This step is called *slicing* and it is one of the unique features that Opa provides.
4. The compiler computes the data schema and generates all database queries.
5. It then translates all client-side code from Opa to JavaScript.
6. Finally, it generates the Opa server-side code to JavaScript code (with the Node.js backend) and embeds the client resources (including the generated client code) so that the server can send them to any client that connects.

Of course, you don't need to know exactly how the Opa compiler works to develop applications. Several development environments (or IDEs) have integrated project build capability, so the compilation process is just a keystroke away.

Throughout this book, we will show you how to work with Opa using the command line, since it works repeatably on all platforms. IDEs are just graphical interfaces for running the same commands for you.

If there are any problems, the compiler will inform you of them with appropriate error or warning messages. Otherwise, an executable JavaScript file will be generated. In this case, it will be called *hello.js*.

Details About the Opa Runtime

The Opa compiler outputs a standard JavaScript application that uses two main technologies:

1. The Node.js framework for the runtime
2. The MongoDB database

Opa-generated apps check that their own runtime environment is correct—that is, that your system is properly installed—so both should be set up by now. If not, check "Installing Opa" (page 3).

You can compile a program without running it by invoking:

```
Tokyo:~ henri$ opa file.opa
```

without the double minus sign.

If you look at what happened in your directory, you will see that Opa creates one file and one directory:

```
Tokyo:~ henri$ ls
_build          program.js      program.opa
```

The *program.js* file is the one you can run by invoking:

```
Tokyo:~ henri$ ./program.js
Http serving on http://localhost:8080
```

The *_build* directory contains the resources of the generated application. The application that results is a standard Node.js/MongoDB application that you can deploy in the cloud.

If some Node.js packages are missing, Opa will guide you through installing them when running your application:

```
Tokyo:~ henri$ opa file.opa
--> some node modules are missing, please run: npm install mongodb formidable
nodemailer imap
```

The cloud platform that most startups use, Amazon EC2, plays nicely with Opa. Go to *https://github.com/MLstate/opalang/wiki/Amazon-Image-for-Opa* for more information. Another interesting option is to use an online platform (a concept also called Platform-as-a-Service, or PaaS) on which you can deploy your application code directly. Platforms such as dotCloud and Heroku support Opa. Please consult *https://github.com/MLstate/opalang/wiki/Opa-in-the-Cloud* for up-to-date instructions for each platform.

Toward Real Programs

In our short "Hello, World" application, all the code went into a single *hello.opa* file. For real programs, you'll want to split the code among different files.

For instance, the popular MVC (Model-View-Controller) approach is to separate three things in an application: the *model*, which represents the data and its treatment; the *view*, which is the user interface of the data; and the *controller*, which synchronizes the model and the view.

It's very easy to start a new application with Opa thanks to a scaffolding mechanism that automatically creates an empty MVC application for you. Just type:

```
Tokyo:~ henri$ opa create myapp
OpaCreate: Generating myapp/Makefile...
OpaCreate: Generating myapp/Makefile.common...
OpaCreate: Generating myapp/opa.conf...
OpaCreate: Generating myapp/resources/css/style.css...
OpaCreate: Generating myapp/src/controller/main.opa...
OpaCreate: Generating myapp/src/model/data.opa...
OpaCreate: Generating myapp/src/view/page.opa...
```

Now you can type:

```
$ cd myapp
$ make run
```

to create a `myapp` application.

You can compile it and run it using the following command:

```
Tokyo:~ henri$ cd myapp; make run
```

To see the source of the application, take a look at the generated files and open *main.opa*, *data.opa*, and *page.opa* with your favorite editor:

```
Tokyo:~ henri$ ls -R src
controller              model           view

src/controller:
main.opa
```

```
src/model:
data.opa

src/view:
page.opa
```

We will discuss the code in Chapter 2, but for now it's important to know the following:

- The controller *main.opa* is the main file of the application, much like *hello.opa* was.
- The model *data.opa* is almost empty and contains a sample database declaration.
- The view *page.opa* is mostly static HTML content.

Battle Plan

Now that you have written your first Opa application, you are ready to proceed with the main goal of this first part of the book: creating a simple wiki app. Our high-level *specification* for the app is as follows:

- The app should support the popular Markdown (*http://en.wikipedia.org/wiki/Markdown*) markup format.
- Different *topics* should correspond to different URLs.
- Editing should be inline, with an easy way to switch between viewing and editing modes.
- It will be rather simple: no preview (in editing mode), no index, and no user and history management (i.e., everyone can edit pages, and the app will not store previous versions of pages, nor information about who made the modifications).

The application is not overly complicated, but it still has a number of interesting features that will give you a great opportunity to learn how to tackle different issues in Opa. In the following chapters, you will learn how to:

- Declare web servers, handle requests to different URLs, and work with resources (Chapter 3)
- Store and manipulate data in a database (Chapter 4)
- Create user interfaces (UIs) based on the HTML and CSS web standards (Chapter 5)

But before you do that, you need to learn a bit more about Opa, which you will do in Chapter 2.

Summary

In this chapter, you got a feel for what Opa is. You learned how to:

- Install Opa
- Write and run a simple app
- Set up your next goal

Opa Fundamentals

In Chapter 1, you wrote your first Opa program. That will always return the same value, Hello, world, as a main title. The value itself is:

```
<h1>Hello, world</h1>
```

This value is an HTML fragment, one of the primitive values of Opa. The second myapp application you saw in Chapter 1 also contains HTML values in *src/view/page.opa*:

```
content =
  <div class="hero-unit">
    Page content goes here...
  </div>
```

Here, the HTML value is named content, so it can be reused later.

 Opa also offers a universal closing tag, </>, that you can use to close any tag. In the previous case, you could have written:

```
content =
  <div class="hero-unit">
    Page content goes here...
  </>
```

Let's discover the Opa values right now.

Primitive Values

As with most programming languages, Opa supports strings, integers, and floats, but Opa also supports native web values such as HTML and CSS elements. As you can see, comments in Opa consist of text preceded by double slashes, //:

```
"hi" // a string
12 // an integer
3.14159 // a float
<p>Paragraph</p> // an HTML fragment
#id // a DOM identifier
css {color: black} // a CSS property
```

HTML values are fragments of HTML5. Each fragment has an opening tag such as <p> and a closing tag such as </p>. The <p> tag is the tag that defines a *paragraph*. We will provide a more complete list of tags shortly, but for now here are the main ones (see Table 2-1):

Table 2-1. Most common tags in HTML5

Tag	Definition
p	Paragraph
h1	Level 1 title (header)
h2..6	Level 2 to 6 title (header)
div	Generic container
span	Inline generic container
ul	List of unnumbered items
li	List item
a	Link
video	Video item

You can embed HTML fragments, as shown here:

```
<div>
  Content <span>button</span>
  <ul>
    <li>First item</li>
    <li>Second item</li>
  </ul>
</div>
```

 Be careful to properly close tags when embedding them: the first one opened should be the last one closed. This is true for all except a handful of tags that don't necessarily need to be closed, such as <meta>, <img>, <input>, and some others.

Tags can have attributes. For instance, the a tag has the href attribute, which specifies the HTML reference it points to. So to insert a link to *http://google.com*, you can write:

```
<a href="http://google.com">Google</a>
```

HTML fragments, when grouped together, create a *document*. We will discuss all the relevant properties of a document in Chapter 5. For now, it's sufficient to know that tags can have a unique ID using the `id` attribute.

For instance, `<div id="iamunique">...</div>` creates an `iamunique` ID that can be accessed by the *DOM identifier* `#iamunique`.

All Opa values can be named, to be reused later in your program. Here is an example:

```
customer = "John Doe"
price = 12.99
tax = price * 0.16
total = price + tax
```

Note that you can play with these basic values by inserting them into the former `Hello, World` application. For instance, try:

```
Server.start(Server.http,
  { title: "Hello, world",
    page: function() {
      customer = "John Doe";
      price = 12.99;
      tax = price * 0.16;
      total = price + tax;
      <p>Customer {customer} has to pay {total}</p>
    }
  }
)
```

Here are a few things to note regarding the preceding code:

- Traditionally, each line of computation ends with a semicolon. There is ongoing debate over whether this is a good thing or not. In Opa, you can omit the semicolons if you want to.
- The end of the computation generates an HTML fragment and uses a mechanism known as *string expansion* to insert values (known as `customer` and `total`) inside the text. As you can see, you use braces for string expansion in Opa.

Dynamic Content

Thus far, you have learned how to build *static content*. Each time you run your application by pointing your browser to *http://localhost:8080*, you get the same content.

The Web was born this way, although originally the mechanism was different, as developers used to write static HTML content within files and used a static server program, such as Apache, to serve the files to users' browsers. The pages would use the HTML `<a>` tag to create links between pages or between different sites.

But we are here to *build applications*. An application consists primarily of web values that can do the following:

- React to the users' actions.
- Store data (e.g., user accounts) permanently in a database.

The most basic user action is the mouse click. Modern applications do not use the link tag to react to users' mouse clicks. So we will use an HTML attribute, onclick, which is present in many tags.

Let's create a small application that displays "Thank you" once the user clicks on "Click me":

```
Server.start(Server.http,
  { title: "Hello, world",
    page: function() {
      <div onclick={function(_) { #thankyou = "Thank you" }}>Click me</div>
      <div id="thankyou"/>
    }
  }
)
```

Run the application now! You should see something similar to Figure 2-1. You can restart your application by refreshing the page in your browser.

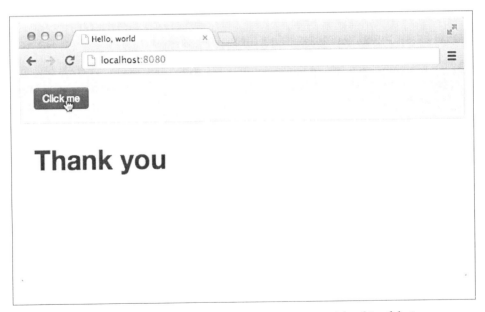

Figure 2-1. The same dynamic application as in Figure 1-1 with a bit of design

The most important new line in this program is:

```
<div onclick={function(_) { #thankyou = "Thank you" }}>Click me</div>
```

which combines two things:

- The HTML value `<div onclick={...}>Click me</div>`
- The resultant *action*, `function(_) { #thankyou = "Thank you"}`

We won't explain every bit of code in that line right now (you will know everything by the end of this chapter), but it is important to note the following:

- You bind Opa code to the `onclick` event with the opening braces.
- You recognize that #thankyou is a DOM identifier value, and you can assign content to the DOM identifier like you do for other values.

To continue our quest, you need to understand two powerful programming mechanisms:

- *Records*, which allow you to structure data
- *Functions*, which help you to organize your application code

It turns out that you are already using both! The record lies behind the following:

```
{ title: ..., page: ... }
```

The function was already used twice:

- For the page that displays by default
- Again, when you click on "Click me"

Records

One of the main features in terms of Opa structuring values is records. As you will see throughout this book, Opa records are extremely powerful and you will use them a lot. Their nickname is "Power Rows."

Records are a set of values, each defined by its *field* name. Values for each field can be of any type, including records or even more complex types:

```
// this is a record with 3 fields
{ first_name: "John", last_name: "Doe", age: 18 }

// this is a record with 2 fields, one of them being a record itself
{ product: "book", price: { base: 29.99, tax: 4.80 } }
```

Naturally, it's useful to name values so that you can construct more complex ones step by step:

```
level1_pricing = { base: 29.99, tax: 4.80 }
book = { product: "book", price: level1_pricing }
```

As we said earlier, all programs, including the very first one you wrote, use records:

```
{ title: "Hello, world",
  page: function() { <h1>Hello, world</h1> }
}
```

The code includes a record that has two fields: title, which is a string, and page, which is another value that we will discuss next.

Records in Opa can be extended, that is, you can add new fields later in your program:

```
level1_pricing = { level1_pricing with total: 29.99 + 4.80}
```

Introduction to Types, and More About Records

Now that you know about basic values and records, it's time to learn more about types. You should be familiar with types. You have seen strings and integers, and as a developer, you know they represent *different* types of values. So does Opa!

```
"Hey" // this has type string
10 // this has type int
```

You can enforce types by writing them if you want, but in most cases, Opa infers them for you and you can safely omit them:

```
string text = "Hey"
```

Opa uses the type information to help you. For instance, Opa won't let you mix different types as doing so is either a bug or a bad coding practice. Try writing:

```
1 + "Hello"
```

and see how Opa reacts.

Often, the mistake is not straightforward and involves two different parts of the code. Opa handles this particularly well. If you write:

```
a = 1;
b = "Hello";
a + b
```

Opa will tell you what the error is and why it occurred. Try it!

You will get the following error message:

```
Error: File "typeerror.opa", line 3, characters 1-5, (3:1-3:5 | 21-25)
Type Conflict
    (1:5-1:5)              int
```

```
(2:5-2:11)          string
```

```
The types of the first argument and the second argument
of function + of stdlib.core should be the same
```

The preceding error message says that:

- 1 is of type `int` (this was inferred).
- "Hello" is of type `string` (this was inferred as well).
- The type error exists in expression `a + b`.
- Both arguments of function + should have the *same* type.

To make it easier to read type error messages, you can name types:

```
type mytype = string
mytype text = "Hey"
```

This becomes useful with records. Each record (as with all other values in Opa) has its corresponding type, even though you will not have to spell it out. For instance:

```
{ title: "The Firm",
  author: { first_name: "John", last_name: "Grisham" } }
```

has type:

```
type book = { string title,
              {string first_name, string last_name} author }
```

which you should read as: "Type `book` is a record with two fields: `title` and `author`. Field `title` has type `string`, whereas `author` is a field whose type is a `record` with two `string` fields: `first_name` and `last_name`."

After such type declaration, you could as well write:

```
book some_book = { title: "The Firm",
                   author: {first_name: "John", last_name: "Grisham"} }
```

In the preceding code, you gave a name (`some_book`) and an explicit type (`book`) to the value shown previously.

Sometimes the expressions describing record fields can get long and complex:

```
author = { first_name: long_expression_to_compute_first_name,
           last_name: long_expression_to_compute_last_name}
```

In this case, to improve readability we will often compute and bind them first:

```
author =
  first_name = long_expression_to_compute_first_name
  last_name = long_expression_to_compute_last_name
  {first_name: first_name, last_name: last_name}
```

For this frequent case where fields are initialized from variables with the same name, Opa provides an *abbreviation* and allows you to replace the last line in the preceding code with:

```
{~first_name, ~last_name}
```

Here {~field, ...} stands for {field: field, ...}. If all fields are constructed in this way, you can even put the *tilde* in front of the record and write:

```
~{first_name, last_name}
```

You will often construct one record from another, as in:

```
grisham = {first_name: "John", last_name: "Grisham"}
steinbeck = {first_name: grisham.first_name, last_name: "Steinbeck"}
```

Opa facilitates this frequent-use case with the following construction:

```
{record with field1: value1, ... fieldN: valueN}
```

The value of this expression is the same as that of `record` except for fields `field1` to `fieldN`, which are given values `value1` to `valueN`. For instance, the `steinbeck` value in the previous code can be replaced with:

```
steinbeck = {grisham with last_name: "Steinbeck"}
```

Records are ever-present in Opa. Their power comes from the fact that all record manipulations are *typechecked*:

- You cannot try to access a field that does not exist.
- You cannot misspell a field's name (or rather, you can, but the compiler will point out your mistake).
- You cannot try to access a field in a type-incompatible way (i.e., as a `string` when it is an `int`).

This power does not cost you anything, as you can just use records as you would in a *dynamic language* without ever explicitly declaring their types.

A Brief Introduction to Variants

One last aspect of the mighty record is *variants*.

Variants are the way to properly represent *multiple-choice lists*. Imagine that you want to define a currency type for an online store that handles payments in US dollars (USD), Canadian dollars (CAN), and British pounds (GBP). You could use the `string` type to define that value. But what if you write the following at some point?:

```
price1 = { amount: 4.99, currency: "USF" }
```

The typo will remain unnoticed, the compiler won't complain, and the related bugs will have to be hunted down during the app testing. As a result, depending on the code structure, the item might not be billed.

Instead, you can write:

```
type currency = { USD } or { CAN } or { GBP }
// here price is a previously defined book value
price = { amount: 29.99, currency: { USD }}
```

The or keyword states that the type currency will be one of the three options: USD, CAN, or GBP. Opa provides very useful *typechecking* for variants. For instance, it checks that values are only allowed variants or that you always take all variants into account. You should use them instead of strings as much as possible.

We will discuss variants in more detail in Chapter 7.

Functions: Building Blocks

Before we move on to the main example of this part of the book, let's take a look at some building blocks of the language that you will need to understand.

Structuring programs is very important. You never want to write your program as a single piece of code; rather, you want to break it down into blocks. The two main block levels are:

- The modules (for bigger applications, which we will take a look at later)
- The functions (inside modules and for any application)

Using functions, you make your program more readable and your code reusable.

Functions are written and called very easily:

```
// the following function computes the tax of a given price
function compute_tax(price) {
  price * 0.16;
}

// we now can call (or invoke) the compute_tax function as much as we want
tax1 = compute_tax(4.99);
tax2 = compute_tax(29.99);
```

Here we have the function keyword, then the name of the function, compute_tax, and a list of its arguments in between parentheses. In this case, there's only one argument: price, followed by the *function body* inside curly braces. Opa does not have an explicit return keyword and instead adopts the convention that the last expression in the function is its return value. Here, it means the function returns the value of price times 0.16.

The open parenthesis in function invocation must immediately follow the function's name, with no spaces in between.

The use of functions in this example means that when the tax level changes, you only have to modify one line of your program, instead of chasing down all the places where the tax is computed in your application. For this reason, you should always use functions whenever you can, and never copy and paste code. Each time you are tempted to copy and paste your code, you should use a function instead.

 You may have noticed that we introduced a *semicolon* at the end of line. This is because we are getting into real programs, which involve several computations. Therefore, we use a semicolon to indicate that a given computation is finished, and that we can proceed to the next one. In many cases, semicolons can be omitted and there is still no consensus on whether it's a good or a bad design decision. You have to find your own coding style!

Functional Programming

The coding style that Opa promotes is called the *functional programming style*. Among other things, this means that *functions* play a central role and are very powerful. The functional programming style is often described as elegant, and we will show you why. But for now, it helps to know that the main difference between functional programming and classic programming is that in the former, values are *not mutable* by default.

For instance, in Opa, the main definition of values such as the following is the binding of a value:

```
name = expression
```

However, this does not create a *variable* in the classic programming style. The previous expression just means we give `name` to the `expression` and can subsequently use `name` to refer to the value denoted by `expression`.

The main reason for this is that immutable code is easier to reason about. In the absence of variables, the result of a function depends only on its arguments. Contrast this with a function whose behavior depends on a bunch of global variables. This is one of the main reasons why in the excellent book *Effective Java* (Addison-Wesley), where mutability is the norm, the author advises that you use immutability whenever possible, explaining:

> There are many good reasons for this: immutable classes are easier to design, implement, and use than mutable classes. They are less prone to error and are more secure.

Our argument for immutability also concerns scaling web applications and services. The architecture prevalent today for scaling up is to use *stateless* servers that can be multiplied without limits. Should a server fail, a new one pops in, and traffic is directed to random servers. But this implies that no application has unsaved data or state. The problem here is that mutable variables often contain such information, and this information will not be synchronized with these other servers unless the synchronization has been done manually (which is a painful process). Therefore, not using state (and variables) is a good programming practice, today more than ever.

Bindings Versus Variables

It is important to understand that value binding is different from variable creation. Variables, as you know them from other programming languages, are *mutable*. This means you can reassign different values to them, such as in this JavaScript snippet:

```
x = 10
f = function() { return x + 1 }
x = 20
f()
```

Here, the value returned is 21, since in JavaScript the function f points to the modified value of the variable x. However, the following Opa snippet returns 11!

```
x = 10
f = function() { x + 1 }
x = 20
f()
```

This is because Opa values are *immutable* and they cannot change subsequently. Therefore, in the preceding Opa snippet, x is being redefined as a new value, but the function f still points to the previous value.

But there's more to it.

Bindings and functions are deeply linked. Let's play with them a bit by writing a function that computes the Euclidean distance between two points:

```
function distance(x1, y1, x2, y2) {
    dx = x1 - x2
    dy = y1 - y2
    Math.sqrt_f(dx*dx + dy*dy)
}
```

In the preceding code, the function distance first binds the value x1-x2 to dx, and similarly binds y1-y2 for dy, and then uses dx and dy in the final expression. Math.sqrt_f is a function from the Math module (more about modules later) of the standard library for computing the square root of a given floating-point number.

In fact, the bindings inside functions can include *local functions*, so the previous could be rewritten as follows, introducing the intermediate sqr function:

```
function distance(x1, y1, x2, y2) {
  dx = x1 - x2
  dy = y1 - y2
  function sqr(x) { x*x }
  Math.sqrt_f(sqr(dx) + sqr(dy))
}
```

Finally, functions can be *anonymous*, in which case they do not have a name but they can be used inside any expression. The anonymous variant of the incr function in the preceding code would be:

```
function(x) { x + 1 }
```

This variant can be stored in a named value:

```
incr = function(x) { x + 1 }
```

Anonymous functions are particularly useful for passing arguments to other functions; for instance, to specify how the app should react to a user's actions.

As you can see, functional programming allows much better control of programming scope. In pure JavaScript, you would write:

```
var foo;
if (x==10) { foo = 20; } else { foo = 30; }
```

This would introduce a variable, and then set its value, even if foo is unmodified in the rest of the program. In Opa, you simply write:

```
foo = if (x==10) { 20; } else { 30; }
```

The preceding code will have the guarantee that foo is not further modified.

Purity, or Not

Languages that prohibit destructive modifications (updates) of their data structures are called *purely functional*. One example of such a language is Haskell.

Opa takes a somewhat more liberal approach, where immutability is the default. Defaults *are* very important, though, as the article *Why the Defaults Matter* (*http://onorioc.word press.com/2012/03/27/why-the-defaults-matter*) convincingly explains for the major part of the language.

But although purely functional languages can be beautiful, they also can be unpractical. In Opa, all database operations, which is the subject of Chapter 4, are mutable. Yes, mutable variables also exist in Opa. We just made it a bit harder for you to use those dangerous features!

Functional + Typed

At the beginning of this chapter, we played with types. Opa is indeed a *statically typed* language. This means that every value has a type assigned to it, and this assignment takes place at compilation time. Being typed is orthogonal to being a functional language. This is important, as the compiler uses this information to detect and report all kinds of flaws in the program.

So why were there no types in the code snippets shown in the preceding section? In Opa, explicitly writing types is often not required as the types are *inferred* in the absence of explicit type annotations. This means you could write the `distance` function with explicit types as follows (the additions are in bold):

```
function float distance(float x1, float y1, float x2, float y2) {
  float dx = x1 - x2
  float dy = y1 - y2
  Math.sqrt_f(dx*dx + dy*dy)
}
```

Arithmetic operators work both for `int` and for `float` types, so the only reason all values are given the `float` type is because of the `Math.sqrt_f` function (its `int` counter-part is called `Math.sqrt_i`).

The *type inference* that the compiler performs may not seem too impressive on this trivial example, but in later chapters, when we deal with more complex types, its benefits will become more pronounced. The type checker algorithm that performs type inference and verification is a very complex and sophisticated algorithm—especially the one in Opa, which required tremendous effort on the part of Opa developers to specify and implement.

Why Static Typing Matters

Many web application development frameworks today rely on dynamically typed programming languages.

One of the key benefits of Opa is that it provides static typing before generating standard JavaScript code. Since the Opa compiler is able to detect a huge class of programming errors, it reports them to the developer even before it runs and tests the application. Due to the very lax nature of JavaScript, such verifications are impossible to perform on pure JavaScript.

Time spent debugging is greatly diminished, and you can be very productive with Opa.

Opa programs are immune to many problems such as *null pointer exceptions, buffer overflows*, and *code injections*. This means the language, out of the box, offers *high security guarantees* thanks to its static typing discipline.

Summary

In this chapter, we learned the fundamental concepts of Opa, in particular:

- How to use records to structure data
- How to write Opa functions
- Why Opa is *functional* and why this is important
- What types str and why they are important

In the next chapter we will talk about servers: how to handle resources and different URLs of an application.

CHAPTER 3

Servers, Resources, and URLs

Applications contain resources (images, scripts, styles, etc.), and they need to navigate between different pages with different URLs. In this chapter, we will explore how to create a more generic application.

Web Resources

A *resource* is anything that can be sent from the server to the client. Figure 3-1 presents different types of web resources, including:

- HTML content
- JavaScript code
- Cascading Style Sheets (CSS)
- Images (in PNG, JPG, or GIF formats)
- XML files

Embedding (Static) Resources

Opa contains directives to embed resources. The simplest one is `@static_resource`:

```
resource logo = @static_resource("img/logo.png")
```

The string given as the argument to this directive is a path to the resource, which can be relative to the directory from which the project will be compiled.

This directive acts as a function; that is, you can bind its result to a variable (here, `logo`) and use it in your program. The type of this variable is `resource`, which is an object that can be sent from the server in response to the client's request.

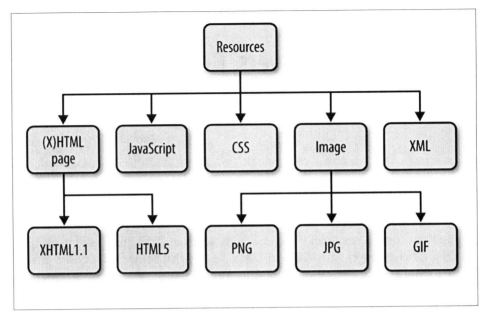

Figure 3-1. Different types of web resources

Sometimes you may have several resources you want to use: for example, a directory full of images. Instead of including each image one by one, you can use `@static_resource_directory`:

```
resources = @static_resource_directory("resources")
```

This line of code will include all resources based on all files from a given directory (here, `resources`) and its subdirectories.

What is the type of this variable? Such an embedded directory is represented as a mapping from filenames (`string`) to resources (`resource`), and hence has the type `map(string, resource)`. We will talk more about maps in "Maps (Dictionaries)" (page 38).

> The counterparts of those two directives are `@static_content` and `@static_content_directory`, and they expose the *content* of the external files without wrapping them up as resources.

Serving Resources

Embedding resources is the first step. The next step is to instruct the web server to serve them for certain requests. Remember the `Server.start` function and how you used it in your first Opa app in "Writing and Running the Code" (page 4)? The second argument defines how different requests should be handled. To serve resources from the *resources* directory you first need to embed them:

```
resources = @static_resource_directory("resources")
```

Now you need to create a server for them:

```
Server.start(Server.http, {resources: resources})
```

Note that before you used a `{title: ..., page: ...}` variant for this second argument to create a single-page app, that is, to direct all client requests to `page`. This new variant, `{resources: ...}`, creates a server that just responds to requests for `resources`.

Imagine that the local *resources* directory has the following structure:

```
+- resources
   +- imgs
   |  +- opa-logo.png
   +- css
   |  +- style.css
```

In this case, running the preceding application and directing the browser to *http://localhost:8080/resources/css/style.css* would give you the stylesheet. What if you tried some other URL? This would result in the infamous "`Error 404: Not Found`" error.

OK, so what if you wanted to extend your "Hello web" application slightly and use some resources in it? You could use two servers:

```
// serve resources
Server.start(Server.http, {resources: @static_resource_directory("resources")})

// serve the main page
function page() {
  <img src="resources/img/logo.png" alt="Opa"/>
  <hr/>
  <h1>This is a demo of a very simple Opa app.</h1>
}
Server.start(Server.http, { title: "Hello web", page: page })
```

Note how this code combined the directive to embed the resources and the server declaration in one; this is entirely permissible.

What happens if you declare more than one server? For every request, the servers will be tried one by one. If a request can be handled by the resources server, it handles it. Otherwise, the request will be handed over to the second server, which in this case can handle each and every request.

 Be aware that the order of the servers *does* matter. If you swapped the declarations, all URLs would be handled by your "one page server" and hence no resources would ever be served.

Another way to achieve the same effect is to simply use a list of servers in the second argument of Server.start. In this case, the preceding program could be written more concisely as:

```
function page() {
  <img src="resources/img/logo.png" alt="Opa"/>
  <hr/>
  <h1>This is a demo of a very simple Opa app.</h1>
}
Server.start(Server.http,
  [ { resources: @static_resource_directory("resources") },
      { register: {css:["/resources/css/style.css"]} },
    { title: "Database Demo", page: page }
  ]
)
```

 In the preceding code, we used *square brackets* to introduce the list. Therefore, each list item is inside the *curly braces*, separated from the others by a *comma*.

Now compile your application:

```
Demo:~ ida$ opa simple_demo.opa
```

And run it:

```
Demo:~ ida$ ./simple_demo.js
Http serving on http://Demo.local:8080
```

When you open it in the browser, you will see input similar to that shown in Figure 3-2, which has a little CSS file included.

 You will learn how to use embedded CSS stylesheets in "Adding Style (CSS)" (page 51), where we will talk about creating user interfaces.

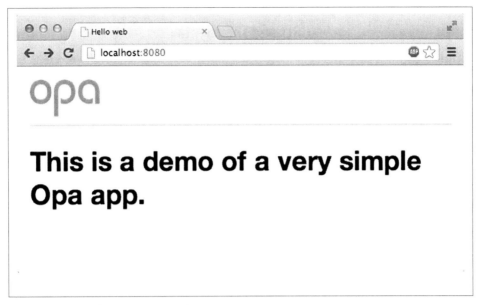

Figure 3-2. Our first program with resources

Constructing (Dynamic) Resources

In addition to embedding static, ready-to-use resources, it is also possible to create them on the fly. You will rarely do this for such things as images and stylesheets, but you will often do this to create HTML pages dynamically; for example, pages based on the state of the database or on user input.

Opa offers many functions for this; the ones we will typically use are:

```
xhtml Resource.page(string title, xhtml body)
xhtml Resource.styled_page(string title, list(string) stylesheets, xhtml body)
```

`Resource.page` takes two parameters, `title` and `content`, and constructs a page resource with this data. `Resource.styled_page` is similar, but it takes one extra argument: a list of URLs of CSS stylesheets to be used to style the application. You will see an example of how to use it in the following section.

URL Dispatching

All the applications you have developed so far have consisted of just a single page, but in practice most bigger sites will have multiple pages. The standard way to handle this is with *Uniform Resource Locators*, more commonly known as *URLs*.

With what you've learned so far, it is very easy to build sites consisting of multiple pages. You can do this via yet another variant of the argument accepted in the Server.start function: {dispatch: dispatch_fun}, where dispatch_fun is a function that takes a *structured URL* as an argument and produces a resource to deliver to the user. This process is often referred to as *URL dispatching*.

You learned about resources in "Web Resources" (page 27) and about how to create them dynamically in "Constructing (Dynamic) Resources" (page 31). But what is a *structured URL*? It is a structural representation of a URL with all its components separated. Since your application will work within a single domain, you are working with *relative URLs* here, or URLs relative to the domain of the application, without the scheme and domain parts.

Here is the definition of the type representing such URLs in Opa:

```
type Uri.relative =
  { list(string) path,
    list((string, string)) query,
```

```
    option(string) fragment,
    bool is_directory,
    bool is_from_root }
```

The preceding code consists of the following:

- A path split into a list of directories separated by a slash (/)
- A query consisting of a list of pairs of key-value associations
- An optional fragment (we will discuss options in more detail later)
- is_from_root and is_directory, which denote, respectively, whether the string representation of the path starts or ends with a slash (/)

For example, consider the following address within a website:

```
/over/there/index.html?type=animal;name=ferret#nose
```

The structured representation of this address in Opa will be:

```
{ path: ["over", "there", "index.html"],
  query: [("type", "animal"), ("name", "ferret")],
  fragment: some("nose"),
  is_from_root: true,
  is_directory: false }
```

Due to HTTP, the fragment identifier is not transmitted from the client to the server via a normal web request.

To practice URL dispatching in Opa, let's write a simple program that will construct a page consisting of the relative address requested by the user. If that address refers to a path starting with bold, the remaining part of the address will be printed in **bold**. If it starts with italic, it will be shown in *italic*.

Hopefully, the following short program should not be too difficult to understand now:

```
function start(url) {
  match (url) {
    case {path: ["bold" | text] ... }:
      Resource.page("Bold", <b>{text}</b>)
    case {path: ["italic" | text] ...}:
      Resource.page("Italic", <i>{text}</i>)
    case {~path ...}:
      Resource.page("Regular", <>{path}</>)
  }
}

Server.start(Server.http, {dispatch: start})
```

Summary

In this chapter you learned how to deal with URLs and resources in Opa. Specifically, you learned:

- What web resources are
- How to embed them in an Opa server
- How to serve resources to application users
- How to create dynamic HTML resources
- How to dispatch URLs, that is, serve different content for different URLs

In the next chapter you will learn about data storage, or how to permanently store some application data in a database.

CHAPTER 4

Data Storage

Opa manages all aspects of applications and services within a single language semantic. Storing and querying data is, not surprisingly, one of the core features of Opa.

In most frameworks, we use APIs and connectors to communicate between the language and a database. Both of these "speak different languages," with some form of mapping in between them.

The Opa approach is slightly different, with the database operations being very tightly integrated into the language and the mapping being performed fully transparently by the compiler. The layer that performs transparent mapping of data is known as *DbGen*.

In this chapter you will learn about Opa's approach to storing basic types. Then we will discuss how to handle a slightly more complex data type: maps.

CRUD (Create, Read, Update, and Delete)

To get started, let's look at a very simple database declaration, containing only a single `int`, a counter of sorts:

```
database db {
    int /counter = 0;
}
```

As you can see, Opa features a `database` block with a given name and a list of declarations of database values enclosed in curly braces.

 Opa programs can handle multiple database connections, even through different database engines. At the time of this writing, support of MongoDB is much more advanced, but CouchDB is also supported and PostgreSQL support is in progress.

Every declaration consists of a type (here, `int`), a *path* (here, `/counter`), and optionally, a *default value* (here, `0`).

The default value is used when you attempt to read a path's value that does not exist. In cases where the path was never written or was removed, the default value is returned.

 Omitting initialization values will cause Opa to use a default value, which is `0` for `int`, `0.0` for `float`, and `""` for `string` values.

Locations in Opa's database are called *paths*, as they bear a strong similarity to filesystem paths. Every value is available at a path consisting of the database name, followed by the path of the value, in our case `/db/counter`. You can read a given value by simply writing its path, as in:

```
counter_value = /db/counter
```

 There is an alternative read operation, prefixed with a question mark: `?/db/counter`. The difference occurs in read operations on paths that were never written into. The regular variant in this case will just supply the default, whereas an operator prefixed with a question mark returns *optional* value, with the value present only if it was explicitly written into the path. You will learn more about optional values in Opa in "Polymorphic Types" (page 75).

Similarly, you can write the value using `path <- value` notation:

```
/db/counter <- 42;
```

A few extra operators are also available for manipulating `int` paths:

```
/db/counter++;
/db/counter += 10;
/db/counter -= 3;
```

The last element in CRUD is *Delete*, which is also very easy with Opa. To delete the counter, you write:

```
Db.remove(@/db/counter)
```

Of course, this is just the beginning of the "database story" in Opa. You will learn more as we go along.

To illustrate the usage of the database, let's extend our simple Opa program from "Writing and Running the Code" (page 4) and add a database to it. We'll also use a function that involves the `onclick` attribute from "Dynamic Content" (page 15) to count clicks.

```
database int /counter = 0;
function action(_) {
    /counter++;
    #msg = <div>Thank you, user number {/counter}!</div>
}
function page() {
    <h1 id="msg">Hello</h1>
    <a onclick={action}>Click me</a>
}
Server.start(Server.http,
  [ { resources: @static_resource_directory("resources") },
    { register: {css:["/resources/css/style.css"]} },
    { title: "Database Demo", page: page }
  ]
)
```

Compile and run this application in your terminal:

```
Demo:~ ida$ opa opa_database_demo.opa --
```

You will get a result similar to the screenshot shown in Figure 4-1.

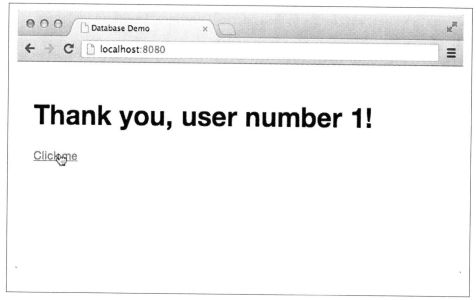

Figure 4-1. Opa database demo app

You will learn more about databases in the following chapters. But first, let's take a look at maps.

Maps (Dictionaries)

The data model for the wiki app you will build is quite simple: you want a collection of *topics*. A topic is represented by a `string` and it should be associated with *content*. You will use the *Markdown markup* format for the content. We will explain how to handle this format in "Markdown" (page 50), but for now, all you need to know is that Markdown is internally represented as a `string`.

For your data model you need a mapping from strings (topics) to strings (Markdown content). This is what *maps* are for.

Map is an abstract data type that associates *keys* with *values*. It is often called a *dictionary* or an *associative array*, and is, in many programming languages, implemented using *hash tables*.

All you need to know for now is that in Opa, the type of the dictionary is `map(key, val)`, where `key` is the type of keys and `val` is the type of values. For instance, `map(int, string)` is a type of dictionary mapping `int` keys to `string` values.

In memory, it is simple to play with maps. The only thing to remember is that they are used in a functional way [for a refresher, refer to "Functional Programming" (page 22)].

You can, for example, store values in successive versions of maps and retrieve them like so:

```
m0 = Map.empty
m1 = Map.add(1, "Paris", m0)
m2 = Map.add(2, "London", m1)

// result is an option
result = Map.get(2, m2)
value = Option.default("Not found", result)
```

Note that although m0, m1, and m2 are separate values, they point to one another and the final data structure is stored efficiently in memory.

Storing maps in databases is even easier than manipulating them in memory, thanks to the DbGen automation layer that Opa provides. For the wiki, you will want a database mapping from strings to strings, which you can obtain with the following declaration:

```
database wiki {
  map(string, string) /page
}
```

The read/write notation that we discussed earlier has a variation that allows you to easily index a given map element by providing its key in *square brackets*. So read and write operations on maps become:

```
Paris_content = /wiki/page["Paris"]    // read
/wiki/page["Paris"] <- Paris_content   // write
```

At this point, you know enough to write two useful functions for data manipulation in the wiki; `save_data(topic, source)` saves `source` as new content for `topic`:

```
function save_data(topic, source) {
  /wiki/page[topic] <- source;
}
```

And `load_data(topic)` retrieves content for `topic`:

```
function load_data(topic) {
  /wiki/page[topic];
}
```

What will happen when you try to load data for a nonexisting page? Remember our discussion about default values in "CRUD (Create, Read, Update, and Delete)" (page 35)? This notion extends to maps as well: if you ask for nonexisting data, you will get the default value, which is an empty string.

It is possible to change this default value, although the syntax will be slightly different, as you would be providing a default for an *individual element* in a map, not the map itself. You will need to add a new line in your database definition:

```
/page[_] = "This page is empty. Double-click to edit."
```

 The underscore (_) here means "any value." We will demonstrate more uses of the underscore later in the book.

The final database declaration for the wiki app looks like this:

```
database wiki {
  map(string, string) /page
  /page[_] = "This page is empty. Double-click to edit."
}
```

Summary

In this chapter you learned the basics of handling data storage in Opa. You should now know how to:

- Store and manipulate basic values in the database
- Store maps, or associations from keys to values

In the following chapter we will look in more detail at the topic of utilizing HTML and CSS to build user interfaces (UIs) in Opa.

CHAPTER 5

Building the UI in HTML and CSS

In this chapter we will focus on building the user interface. The first step is to create the presentation layer in Opa.

HTML Markup

For presentation, Opa uses the modern web standards HTML5 and CSS3 [we will discuss these in more detail in "Adding Style (CSS)" (page 51)]. You already saw a glimpse of how Opa deals with HTML in "Writing and Running the Code" (page 4) and we will expand on that here.

Tags and Attributes

Recall from our earlier discussion that HTML can be included verbatim in Opa programs, and that it can be returned from functions as shown here:

```
function sample_page() {
  <header>
    <h3>HTML in Opa</h3>
  </header>
  <article>
    <div class="container">
      <p>Learning by examples.</p>
    </div>
  </article>
}
```

Now, there are few things to keep in mind when writing HTML snippets in Opa code:

- The name of the closing tag is optional, so `<tag>...</tag>` can be shortened to `<tag>...</>`.
- If the attribute consists of a single string with no special characters (i.e., it consists of only letters, digits, and an underscore) the quotes around it can be omitted.
- Double quotes (as in `attr="..."`) are required; single quotes (as in `attr='...'`) are *not*.

When you apply the first two rules in this list, you can rewrite the preceding snippet as follows:

```
function sample_page() {
  <header>
    <h3>HTML in Opa</>
  </>
  <article>
    <div class=container>
      <p>Learning by examples.</>
    </>
  </>
}
```

Opa also features web templates, known as *markdown* templates, in its standard library.

Inserts

We've discussed the basics of static HTML, but things get much more interesting when you have to generate the HTML programmatically. In Opa, this is mainly achieved using *inserts*, which we will explain now.

If you happen to know JavaScript (do not worry if you don't) you are used to writing code like this:

```
x + " + " + y + " = " + (x+y);
```

Opa's equivalent is the following:

```
"{x} + {y} = {x+y}";
```

This is both shorter and more readable. The parts of the string between the curly braces `{...}` are the expressions that are evaluated, converted to strings (more on the rules for converting to strings later), and inserted at those points in the string literal. This mechanism is easy, readable, and quite importantly, safe, as before "injecting" the computed value it automatically gets properly escaped depending on the object you are inserting to.

This is because inserts work not only on strings, but also, for instance, in HTML fragments. Therefore, you could rewrite the `sample_page` function by first writing a generic function to generate page markup:

```
function gen_page(header, class, content) {
  <header>
    <h3>{header}</h3>
  </header>
  <article>
    <div class={class}>
      <p>{content}</p>
    </div>
  </article>
}
```

The inferred type of this function is as follows:

```
function xhtml gen_page(xhtml header, string class, xhtml content) { ... }
```

xhtml is the HTML type in Opa. Both header and content are HTML fragments that will be inserted in appropriate places, whereas class is a string identifier.

Now you can rewrite your original sample_page function with a simple call:

```
function sample_page() {
  gen_page(<>HTML in Opa</>, "container", <>Learning by examples.</>)
}
```

The empty tags, <>...</>, in the second and third arguments of this call are used in Opa as HTML text delimiters. This means "string" is a string literal, whereas <>string</> is an HTML literal consisting solely of the string text (with no tags).

The advantage of this approach is that now you have a general-purpose gen_page function that you can reuse throughout your program. Indeed, the ability to easily manipulate HTML and write such general-purpose presentation functions is an important aspect of building user interfaces in Opa. As you will learn in the next section, HTML manipulation encompasses not only content generation, but also interactive aspects of the UI. This means you can use similar techniques to write complete, interactive, reusable UI components. But let's not get ahead of ourselves.

Event Handlers

Now that you know how to write static HTML and how to generate it dynamically, you can change the generated page under certain conditions, such as the state of the database. In this section you will learn how to generate *dynamic* pages, or pages that are changing as a result of such things as user interaction or the passage of time (giving animations).

In HMTL, you can achieve this by means of *event handlers*. You can think of event handlers as a way to execute certain code in response to some *event*.

An *event handler* is a function whose call is triggered by some activity in the user interface. Typical event handlers react to a user clicking on some element within a page (a `click` event), pressing the Enter key (a `newline` event), moving the mouse (a `mousemove` event), or loading the page (a `ready` event).

In Opa, an event handler always has the type `Dom.event -> void`.

You can find more information about event handlers in the online Opa API documentation (*http://doc.opalang.org/api*) by searching for the word "Dom.event".

Let's take a closer look at the following function:

```
function page() {
    <p onclick={clicked}>Click me!</p>
}
```

The `onclick` attribute defines a handler for the `click` event. This event is fired when the user clicks with the left mouse button on the given element of the page. The value of this attribute is the `{clicked}` insert. But the interesting part here is that this insert is a *function* that is called when the event occurs. Such functions are of the following type:

```
function void clicked(Dom.event event) {
    ...
}
```

This function takes a single argument of type `Dom.event`, which carries information about the particular event that triggered the handler. It does not return a value.

`void` is a nonvalue in that it indicates the absence of a value. It is mainly used as a return type for functions that actually do not return anything.

`void` ensures that the handler has the correct type. This information is not necessary, but every event handler needs to have this particular type; that is, a single argument of type `Dom.event` and no return value.

If the handler does not need any information from the `event` argument and hence does not use it (this happens very often with event handlers), the compiler generates a warning. This is beneficial, as not using one of the function arguments is often an indication that something is wrong.

In order to avoid this warning, you can use an argument name that starts with an underscore (_). So you could write the header of this function without including the type information, like so:

```
function clicked(_event) { ... }
```

Or more simply:

```
function clicked(_) { ... }
```

 Variables/arguments with an underscore as their name are *throwaway* values; you do not need them. You will often see them in event handlers and in pattern matching, which we discuss in "Pattern Matching" (page 74).

Note that it is perfectly fine to use anonymous functions for event handlers. If you decide to ignore the event argument, you can rewrite the page function as:

```
function page() {
  <p onclick={function(_) { ... }}>Click me!</>
}
```

Providing function bodies for event handlers usually involves some DOM manipulation, a topic we will tackle in the next section.

DOM Manipulation

The Document Object Model (DOM) is a tree-structure representation of an HTML document. Modifying the DOM is the standard way to manipulate page content.

Opa offers a comprehensive set of operations on the DOM. By far the most common operation is replacing the content of a given DOM element:

```
#id = content
```

In the preceding code, id is an identifier (with no quotes around it) and content is an XHTML expression. The result of this command is to replace the DOM element with the given ID, content.

There are two other variants:

```
#id += content
#id =+ content
```

The first one *prepends* content to the id element (i.e., puts it before the existing content) and the second one *appends* it (i.e., puts it after the existing content).

A multitude of additional DOM manipulation functions are also available.[1] The following list describes the ones that are used most often.

- `Dom.fresh_id()` produces a fresh DOM ID, unique in the (local) page; this is very useful when you dynamically generate some HTML, such as a table based on database content, and you need unique identifiers for generated elements. Note that the `fresh_id` function is not cryptographically secure.

- `string Dom.get_content(dom)` retrieves the content of a given DOM element, usually an input field.

- Similarly, `void Dom.set_content(string content, dom dom)` sets the content of the dom element to `content`.

- `void Dom.give_focus(dom dom)` gives focus to the dom element.

- `void Dom.show(dom dom)` and `void Dom.hide(dom dom)` respectively show and hide a dom element from the page.

Example: A Guessing Game

To illustrate the use of event handlers and DOM manipulations, let's modify the program from "Writing and Running the Code" (page 4) to play the following simple game:

1. The computer selects a number x between 1 and 10.

2. The user tries to guess what that number is.

3. The user clicks on the page to reveal the number.

The main function of this program could look as follows:

```
function page() {
  <h1>Guess what is the number between 1 and 10 I'm thinking of?</h1>
  <div id=#response onclick={show_number}>Click to find out!</div>
}
```

The last line of this function constructs a paragraph that reacts to clicks by invoking the following `show_number` function:

```
function show_number(_) {
  #response = <>I was thinking of {1 + Random.int(10)}</>
}
```

`Random.int(x)` is a standard library function that generates a random number between 0 (inclusive) and x (exclusive). Hence, `1 + Random.int(10)` produces the desired random number between 1 and 10.

---

1. The Dom module of Opa contains more than 100 different functions.

So when the user clicks on the text paragraph containing the instructions, he will see a random number that the computer has "selected." Note that the computer chooses the number *after* the user comes up with his number, that is, the first and second steps of the game are reversed in this scenario. But since computers are not yet capable of reading people's minds, this is an unlikely cause for cheating.

Now all you have to do is to start a server, using `Server.start`, and you'll end up with the following complete app. Compare it with your first program from "Writing and Running the Code" (page 4) and note how the `page` function is used instead of an anonymous function; now change the layout to put that declaration on one line. Note that the syntax ~page is just a shortcut for `page: page`, a concept known as *syntactic sugar.*

```
function show_number(_) {
    #response = <>I was thinking of {1 + Random.int(10)}</>
}

function page() {
    <h1>Guess what is the number between 1 and 10 I'm thinking of?</h1>
    <div id=#response onclick={show_number}>Click to find out!</div>
}

Server.start(Server.http, { title: "Guess", ~page })
```

Before we move on to discussing the wiki interface, let's make this game a bit more fun to play. Let's make it a multiple-choice game, and provide hints if we can't find the right number. To do this, start by modifying the UI:

```
<h1>Guess what is the number I'm thinking of</>
<input id=#guess/>
<span onclick={show}>Check</>
<div id=#message/>
```

Rename `#response` to `#message` since several messages might be displayed, and add an *input* to allow the user to enter data. In the previous example, a number was drawn just before it was displayed. You can't do that here, as a number needs to be drawn each time the page is rendered. Hence, at the beginning of the function `page`, you need to create a new `secret` value:

```
secret = 1 + Random.int(10);
```

Then you have to modify the `show` function to compute the right message:

```
message =
    if (guess==secret) { <span class="success">Congrats! < /span> }
    else if (guess<secret) { <>More than this</> }
    else { <>Less than this</> };
```

Note that instead of using the empty HTML tags, you can insert a special span element around the text that is displayed when the user wins, but you should keep the interface as simple as you can in other scenarios.

To pass the secret value to the show function you add it as the first argument:

```
function show(secret, _) {
  ...
}
function page() {
  ...
  <span onclick={show(secret, _)}>Check</>
  ...
}
```

Finally, you need to read the value from the input in the show function and display the result in the #message element. Let's try to do that with the following code:

```
function show(secret, _) {
  guess = Dom.get_value(#guess);
  message = ...
  #message = message;
}
```

This should result in a type error message. This occurs because the guess value read from input is a string whereas secret is an integer. You can resolve this problem by casting the value using:

```
guess = String.to_int(Dom.get_value(#guess));
```

Here's the complete code example:

```
function show_number(_) {
  #response = <>I was thinking of {1 + Random.int(10)}</>
}

function page() {
  <h1>Guess what is the number between 1 and 10 I'm thinking of?</h1>
  <div id=#response onclick={show_number}>Click to find out!</div>
}

Server.start(Server.http, { title: "Guess", ~page })
```

The Wiki Interface (HTML)

Now we are ready to write the user interface part of the wiki app. In this section you will write a display function that takes a single argument, topic, and constructs a page for it. We will assume that you have at your disposal the following functions for data storage, which we discussed in Chapter 4:

- load(topic), which gives the Markdown source associated with topic
- save(topic, source), which associates source with topic

The main idea is that the page can have two modes:

- *Editing*, where the user can edit the content of the page (using Markdown)
- *Display mode*, where the content is just displayed (with appropriate Markdown rendering)

In this example you will have elements for both modes always present on the page, but only one mode will be visible at a time and the other one will be hidden. Dynamically changing the content would also work, but since you did that already in "Example: A Guessing Game" (page 46), let's try this approach now.

HTML Plumbing

This is how the display function, parameterized by wiki page title, topic, will look:

```
function display(topic) {
  content = render(load_data(topic));
  xhtml =
    <header>
      <h3>OpaWiki</h3>
    </header>
    <article>
      <h1>About {topic}</h1>
      <div id=show_container>
        <small><strong>Tip:</strong> Double-click on the content to start
editing it.</small>
        <section id=content_show ondblclick={function(_) { edit(topic) }}>
{content}</section>
      </div>
      <div id=edit_container hidden>
        <small><strong>Tip:</strong> Click outside of the content box to save
changes.</small>
        <textarea id=content_edit rows=30 onblur={function(_) { save(topic) }}/>
      </div>
    </article>;
  Resource.page("About {topic}", xhtml);
}
```

First, we retrieve the content page by loading its data, load_data(topic), and passing it to the render function, which turns a Markdown string into its HTML representation.

Then the page's main HTML is stored in the xhtml value. Here we have a <header> with the name of the application, Opa-wiki. Following that is the wiki article, <article>, consisting of an <h1> heading with a topic name and two <div>s for two application modes, both containing a paragraph (p) with a short explanation. The first <div>

contains a section, `<section>`, for display mode, and the second one contains an editable text box, `<textarea>`, for editing mode. We assign identifiers, `ids`, to both elements and to the `<div>`s, as we will need to refer to them later. Both elements have *event* handlers attached. The static text on the double mouse click (`ondblclick`) will switch us to editing mode, and the editable text when losing focus (`onblur`)—which may occur, for example, as a result of the user clicking outside the box—will switch us back to display mode.

Finally, the last line of this function turns this HTML into a resource, as we discussed in "Web Resources" (page 27).

Markdown

We need to write the `render` function that transforms the Markdown source into a ready-to-display HTML fragment.

 Markdown is a lightweight markup language, which is perfect for obtaining richly formatted user input. You can learn more about its syntax on the original project page (*http://daringfireball.net/projects/markdown/*) or by taking a look at a very nicely done online Markdown editor, *http://dillinger.io*.

As with many other useful projects, Opa has a readily available library for dealing with Markdown. All you have to do is to import it:

```
import stdlib.tools.markdown
```

You will learn more about imports and packaging in Opa in "Packages" (page 83). For now, all you need to know is that this makes the `Markdown` module available to you and that with it you can create the following function:

```
function xhtml xhtml_of_string(Markdown.options options, string source)
```

This takes Markdown source and rendering options and produces an XHTML representation of the source. There is also a `Markdown.default_options` value of type `Markdown.options`, so the `render` function simply becomes:

```
function render(markdown) {
  Markdown.xhtml_of_string(Markdown.default_options, markdown);
}
```

Dynamically Updating the Page

Now let's take a look at the `edit` and `save` functions.

Calling the `edit` function results in a change from display mode to editing mode:

```
function edit(topic) {
  Dom.set_value(#content_edit, load_data(topic));
  Dom.hide(#show_container);
  Dom.show(#edit_container);
  Dom.give_focus(#content_edit);
}
```

In the first line of the preceding code, we set the content of the text editing box to the Markdown source for the current topic, which we fetch with `load_data`. Then we hide the presentation field, display the editing box, and finally, give it a focus.

Similarly, the `save` function switches from edition mode to display mode, saving all the changes the user has made:

```
function save(topic) {
  content = Dom.get_value(#content_edit);
  save_data(topic, content);
  #content_show = render(content);
  Dom.hide(#edit_container);
  Dom.show(#show_container);
}
```

In the preceding code, first we bind `content` to the text the user has entered, and then we save it and use its rendered version for display. Finally, we switch the visibility of the display/editing elements.

Adding Style (CSS)

A close companion of HTML is CSS, which stands for *Cascading Style Sheets*. Whereas HTML is used to describe the *content* and *structure* of web pages, CSS takes care of *presentation semantics* (i.e., appearance and formatting). Knowledge of CSS will help you create more beautiful pages, although you will learn how to style pages without writing CSS yourself in "Bootstrap: Nice, Out-of-the-Box Styling" (page 54). Still, a basic working knowledge of CSS comes in handy in the web world, so we suggest that you learn the basics of CSS.

In Opa, you can work with CSS in three ways:

- Via the usual `style` attribute
- Using Opa's data type and special syntax for CSS
- Using external stylesheets

In addition to discussing these three methods of working with CSS, in this section we will explain how to add some style to the wiki.

Explicit Style Attributes

The first way to use CSS in Opa is with the usual `style` attribute, as follows:

```
function page() {
  <p style="color: white; background: blue; padding: 10px;">Click me</>
}
```

Although this method is supported, its use is discouraged. First, the purpose of CSS is to separate the presentation from the content, and indeed, it is best to do this by writing CSS in an external file, separate from the HTML document. You will learn how to do that in "External CSS" (page 53).

Sometimes, however, the CSS needs to be manipulated dynamically depending on some application logic. Let's take a look at a method that is appropriate in those circumstances.

Opa-Powered Style

Just as Opa offers a data type and special syntax for HTML, it also does so for CSS. The syntax consists of the `css` keyword and the usual CSS syntax within curly braces. For instance, the `page` function you just wrote can be rewritten as:

```
function page() {
  style = css { color: white; background: blue; padding: 10px;}
  <p style={style}>Click me</>
}
```

Here it is without the intermediate binding:

```
function page() {
  <p style={css { color: yellow; background: blue; padding: 10px;}}>Click me</>
}
```

One of the advantages of this over using a string literal for `style` is that the Opa compiler will check such definitions, ruling out syntactic and some semantic mistakes; for instance, `style={css {color: 10px}}` will not be accepted.

 As of this writing, Opa only supports a subset of the CSS3 standard. If your declaration is rejected and you believe it to be correct, chances are it is not yet supported, in which case, you will need to use one of the other two methods for working with CSS in Opa.

There are other advantages of using the Opa compiler. One is that CSS is a data type, and it is possible to parameterize functions by styling information:

```
function paragraph(style, content) {
  <p style={style}>{content}</>
}
```

What is the type of this function?

```
function xhtml paragraph(css_properties style, xhtml content)
```

The type of a single CSS declaration is called `css_properties`.

Another interesting option is to alter the CSS depending on some application logic as, for instance, in the following function:

```
function xhtml block(Css.size width, Css.size height, xhtml content) {
  style = css { width: {width}; height: {height} }
  <div style={style}>{content}</>
}
```

In this declaration you can see the `Css.size` type that denotes the CSS size declaration. There are several other types for CSS notations, including fonts, colors, and background properties.

External CSS

In Chapter 3 you learned how to embed resources in the Opa server. Those resources can include regular external CSS files, and you can instruct Opa to use such CSS as follows:

```
Server.start(Server.http,
  [ {resources: @static_resource_directory("resources")},
    {register: {css:["/resources/css/style.css"]} },
    ...
  ]
)
```

The `css` field of the `register` record contains a list of URLs of CSS files to be used. These files will be used for *all* the pages in the application. It is also possible to use stylesheets on a per-page basis if needed--for instance, with the`Resource.styled_page` function that we discussed in "Constructing (Dynamic) Resources" (page 31):

```
function page_with_style(body) {
  Resource.styled_page("This is a page with style",
  ["resources/custom_style.css"], body)
}
```

Wiki with Style

For the wiki application, you just need to add a simple CSS file, *resources/style.css*, to add a bit of presentation information and, more importantly, hide the editing mode container initially:

```
include:code/wiki/resources/style.css[]
```

Now all you are missing is the following server declaration:

```
Server.start(Server.http,
  [ {resources: @static_include_directory("resources")},
    {register: [{doctype: {html5}}, {css: ["/resources/style.css"]}]},
    {dispatch: start}
  ]
);
```

At this point, you should have a complete and ready-to-run wiki. You compile it with:

```
opa wiki.opa
```

And you run it with:

```
thistle $ ./wiki.js
Http serving on http://thistle:8080
```

Now the server is running. Pointing your browser to *http://localhost:8080* should give a result similar to the screenshots shown in Figure 5-1, which show the app in both display mode and editing mode.

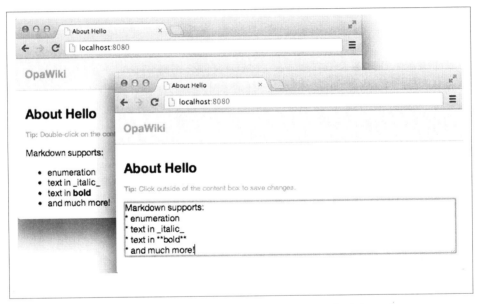

Figure 5-1. Our wiki application in display (left) and editing (right) modes

Bootstrap: Nice, Out-of-the-Box Styling

Typically, web applications are designed by professional web designers. However, in very basic projects, or at the early stages of major projects, a professional web designer may not be readily available. In such cases, you can use a frontend framework such as Bootstrap (*http://twitter.github.com/bootstrap*) for the design task.

Bootstrap is an open source project, developed at Twitter, that provides high-quality, responsive CSS, along with HTML conventions and Java-Script plug-ins for all the typical elements of websites. Using predefined classes and appropriate tagging combinations, developers can obtain a consistent and professional look for their sites for free. Describing Bootstrap itself is beyond the scope of this book, but the project website (*http://bit.ly/Yn6LYe*) is well organized and self-explanatory.

The Opa authors have high regard for this project, and therefore made sure that using Bootstrap in Opa is as easy as it gets. To use Bootstrap in your Opa project, just type a single line:

```
import stdlib.themes.bootstrap
```

This variant imports the latest Bootstrap version supported by Opa.[2] To request a specific version, you can write:

```
import stdlib.themes.bootstrap.v2.1.0
```

Now you can start using Bootstrap-compatible HTML markup and enjoy good-looking pages without any hassle!

In the following code, we will illustrate the power of Bootstrap on the wiki application. All you need to do is replace the xhtml in the display function with the following one, which is using Bootstrap conventions:

```
<div class="navbar navbar-fixed-top">
  <div class=navbar-inner>
    <div class=container>
      <a class=brand href="#">
        Opa Wiki
      </a>
    </div>
  </div>
</div>
<div class=container>
  <h1>About {topic}</>
  <div id=show_container>
    <span class="badge badge-info">Tip</span>
    <small>
      Double-click on the content to start editing it.
    </small>
    <div class="well well-small" id=content_show ondblclick={function(_) { ed-
it(topic) }}>
```

---

2. At the time of this writing it is version 2.2.1.

```
      {content}
    </div>
  </div>
  <div id=edit_container hidden>
    <span class="badge badge-info">Tip</span>
    <small>
      Click outside of the content box to confirm the changes.
    </small>
    <textarea id=content_edit rows=30 onblur={function(_) { save(topic) }} />
  </div>
</div>
```

Once you do that, you no longer need the full CSS we introduced before, and you can replace it with the following:

```
include:code/wiki/resources/style_additional.css[]
```

This code only hides the *editing container*, adds a little extra space between elements, and makes the editing text area the full width of your screen. This uses much simpler CSS yet produces a much more pleasant result, as you can see in Figure 5-2.

Bootstrap offers even more than this screenshot can capture, including responsive design; that is, web pages that display nicely on most devices and screen sizes. As mobile browsers become increasingly important, you will *want* to build responsive applications!

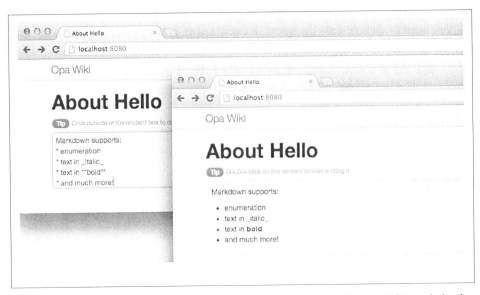

Figure 5-2. Our wiki application with Bootstrap styling in editing (left) and display (right) modes

Working with Designers

We have been lucky to have a UX and UI designer in-house at MLstate. This section is a Q&A with Ida Swarczewskaja, who gives us her best tips on how to work with design and designers when coding with Opa.

How Should I Use the DOM Structure?

The DOM structure should remain light. Try to avoid using too many levels.

Can You Describe Your Development Environment?

Many great tools are available today. My favorite code editor is Sublime Text 2 (*http://www.sublimetext.com/2*). For even more efficiency in building DOM structures I recommend using Emmet (*https://github.com/sergeche/emmet-sublime*), previously known as ZenCoding, with Sublime Text 2.

How Should I Write CSS with Opa?

You can use CSS with Opa in three different ways, as described in "Adding Style (CSS)" (page 51). The method you choose depends on your project. For prototyping or for a small project, you can use explicit style attributes or Opa-powered style. For bigger projects, the best way to start is to create a separate CSS file that is stored in the *resources* or *assets* directory, as described in "External CSS" (page 53). If you are not familiar with CSS and would like to get good UI results with your app, you should use Twitter Bootstrap (*http://twitter.github.com/bootstrap*), which you can easily import into your Opa file.

Which Tools Should I Use to Write CSS?

You can write CSS manually. However, like most designers currently do, I use CSS preprocessors that generate well-formatted CSS and allow better stylesheet file organization. I recommend the following:

- *less*, available at the less website (*http://lesscss.org/*).
- *sass* or *scss*, available at the sass website (*http://sass-lang.com/*). These are dynamic stylesheet languages (extensions of CSS3) that enable you to use nested rules, variables, mixins, functions, and operations.

 Mixins allow you to reuse variables, properties, and selectors; they are great time-savers while declaring CSS3 properties.

How Do I Improve the CSS Workflow in Opa?

When launching the Opa application on a server, *debug mode* allows for real-time editing of CSS files. It is very convenient when working with designers as it allows a fully integrated workflow.

How Often Should Developers and Designers Interact?

Building a great UI and UX for your app requires interaction among developers and designers. Depending on the project, developers should discuss the DOM structure of the app, nesting rules, the elements' class names, and other details with designers before they start coding, and they should check how everything interacts at each stage of the build process.

What Should Developers Know About CSS?

CSS3 replaces most of the images we were used to creating for UIs. CSS3 is commonly used to generate background gradients and tiles, drop shadow and embossing effects, text shadow effects, rounded corners, and transitions. Use `@media queries` for the web apps where responsive cross-platform design is required. Once again, Twitter Bootstrap provides an easy-to-use UI kit for styling responsive grids, navbars, forms, buttons, and other elements. All you have to do is stick to the default as much as possible if you do not want to dig into design.

What Should Designers Know About Opa?

Designers should know how to compile Opa apps, which is pretty easy to learn; edit HTML structures; and write CSS code or use CSS preprocessors to generate CSS code. Designers who write CSS are already syntax experts, so although they cannot usually write code, they are detail-oriented when it comes to syntax and should not break things.

Can You Provide Some Tips for Quickly Customizing Your App's Bootstrap-Based UI?

Due to the popularity of Bootstrap, more and more applications are using it, and hence these applications look the same. I believe every product needs a custom design, though. So here are my tips for developers willing to customize their Bootstrap-based UI:

- The first thing to change is the font. Bootstrap uses Helvetica, which is a very basic font. I suggest changing the font to one that is fancier. For example, the Google Web Fonts Library (*http://www.google.com/webfonts*) has hundreds of free, open source fonts, optimized for use on the Web. If you like Helvetica, you might want to change the font only on the headings and branding elements.

- Another thing that helps to customize your Bootstrap-based UI is changing the default color scheme. You can find great color inspiration on websites like Colour-lovers (*http://www.colourlovers.com/colors*). Pick up some fresh colors and add them to your stylesheet! You can do this directly on the Bootstrap website (*http://twitter.github.com/bootstrap/customize.html#variables*). Alternatively, you can create an additional CSS file and overwrite the CSS properties of the Bootstrap components you are using. This stylesheet should be called after the Boostrap CSS.

- A third way you can quickly customize your app is by adding some texture. Bootstrap has a solid white background. A discrete texture might add some personality to your app, though. Why not choose a free background texture from, for example, the Subtle Patterns website (*http://subtlepatterns.com/*). Retina-resolution images are also provided.

We will demonstrate these tips in action in our bigger application.

Summary

In this chapter you learned how to build user interfaces; in particular, how to:

- Build page content with HTML
- Add style to pages with CSS
- Use Bootstrap to generate nice-looking pages out-of-the-box

At this point, you have completed your simple wiki application and learned a lot along the way.

In Part II of this book you will develop a micro-blogging application, similar to Twitter, though without all the bells and whistles. This will be a great opportunity to learn more advanced topics. Ready? Let's get started!

PART II
Coding a Mini-Twitter

Congratulations on building your first real application in Opa. You now are ready for something bigger! Part II focuses on an application that is a mini micro-blogging platform we call "Birdy." Any resemblance to a well-known micro-blogging platform is purely coincidental!

In this part of the book you will learn how to enable users to post messages that are limited to 140 characters; create sign-up and sign-in forms; create a rich UI for editing messages; parse messages for mentions and hash tags; ensure real-time apparition of messages; and more!

But before we start, let's discuss one of the core features of Opa: *real-time messaging*. In doing so, we will take you through the process of building what might be considered the *core* of a micro-blogging app: a web chat.

CHAPTER 6

The Web Chat App

The simplest example of a real-time web app is a *web chat*, similar to Facebook chat. As real-time is a feature of our micro-blogging app, we detail here what has become the de facto example of Opa programming.

Our goal here is to build the application shown in Figure 6-1: a single chat room. Users connect to chat using regular web browsers, join the room immediately, and can start discussing in real time. For the sake of simplicity, we will choose names of users randomly. We will discuss in Chapter 8 how to add proper user management.

> In the web world, *real time* refers to the ability of a web page to update itself automatically when some data changes. Often in Web 2.0 apps, this is linked to displaying user interactions in real time; that is, updating the user interface of one user when another user does something.

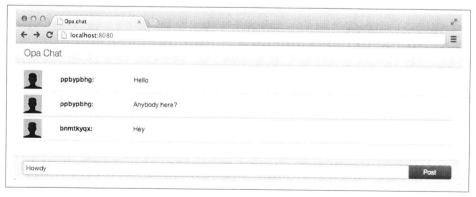

Figure 6-1. Our chat goal

Starting a New Project

To start the new chat application, simply write:

```
Tokyo:~ henri$ opa create chat
```

This will create a chat directory and generate a scaffolding for a new Opa app, with the following content:

```
+- chat
| +- Makefile
| +- Makefile.common
| +- opa.conf
| +- resources
| | +- css
| | | +- style.css
| +- src
| | +- model.opa
| | +- view.opa
| | +- controller.opa
```

The project includes:

- A *Makefile* file for the project (which can be customized)
- A generic *Makefile.common* file (which usually won't be modified)
- A configuration file, *opa.conf* (which lists all the source files of the project and their dependencies; we'll look at this file in more detail in Chapter 7)
- An example style file, *style.css*
- The source files, following the classic MVC pattern, divided into three sub-directories: *model*, *view*, and *controller*, for the standard three application layers

To compile and run the project, type:

```
Tokyo:~ henri$ cd chat; make run
```

View: Building User Interface

Let's start with the user interface; here we see the *view* part of the application, with which you should already be familiar:

```
module View {

    // View code goes here

    function page_template(content) {
      <div class="navbar navbar-inverse navbar-fixed-top">
        <div class=navbar-inner>
          <div class=container>
            <a class=brand href="#">
```

```
           Opa Chat
         </a>
       </div>
     </div>
   </div>
   <div id=#main>
     {content}
   </div>
}

function default_page() {
  content =
    <div class="hero-unit">
      Page content goes here...
    </div>
  page_template("Default page", content)
}

}
```

The View module has two functions: `page_template`, which contains a generic template for any page, and `default_page`, which uses `page_template` to build a page.

For the chat app, you need to modify the `page_template` and `default_page` functions of the View module (*https://github.com/MLstate/hello_chat/blob/master/src/view.opa*) to obtain the desired look and feel for the app. The template also automatically places a CSS stylesheet in *resources/css/style.css*, which you may want to modify (*https://github.com/MLstate/hello_chat/blob/master/resources/css/style.css*) as well.

Model: Application Logic

Now that you have the skeleton of the user interface in place, it's time to bring it to life by adding application logic. This is the *model* part of the application, in which you define the application data, as well as its manipulation and storage, that you wrote in *src/model.opa*.

A chat app is about communicating messages between users. This means you need to decide what *type* of messages you wish to transmit.

In its minimal form, a message is a record that contains two fields: `author` (which is a `string`, i.e., some text) and `text` (also a `string`):

```
type message = {string author, string text}
```

Now that you know what a message is, you need to figure out how to pass it around to different clients. Opa provides three methods of communication between clients and the server:

- Session (for one-way, asynchronous communication)
- Cell (for two-way, synchronous communication)
- Network (for broadcasting messages to a number of observers)

For the chat application, you have a number of clients connected to the chat room, and they all need to be informed of every message posted; therefore, you will use a network:

```
private Network.network(message) room = Network.cloud("room")
```

This extract creates a *cloud network* (ensuring that it will be shared among all running instances of the application) called "room." The cloud name comes from the world of cloud computing and stresses that the networks can be easily distributed among several servers, although scaling Opa is not yet part of this book.

As is the case with everything in Opa, networks have a type. The type of this network is `Network.network(message)`, which means this is a network used to transmit data of type `message`.

By declaring this value as `private`, you ensure that it is not accessible from outside the `Model` and that other functions need to be used to manipulate it. This concept, known as *encapsulation* or *information hiding*, is crucial for writing modular, well-designed programs. We will discuss this further in "Packages" (page 83).

You will need two such functions: one to broadcast a message to all clients and another one to register a callback, which will be invoked whenever a new message has been posted:

```
function broadcast(message) {
  Network.broadcast(message, room);
}

function register_message_callback(callback) {
  Network.add_callback(callback, room);
}
```

Both functions simply invoke relevant features from the `Network` module.

Finally, you need a function to assign usernames to newly connected users. As mentioned earlier, you will simplify the app by choosing those names at random:

```
function new_author() {
  Random.string(8);
}
```

The complete source of the model follows:

```
type message = { string author
               , string text
               }
```

```
module Model {

  private Network.network(message) room = Network.cloud("room")

  exposed function broadcast(message) {
    Network.broadcast(message, room);
  }

  function register_message_callback(callback) {
    Network.add_callback(callback, room);
  }

  function new_author() {
    Random.string(8);
  }

}
```

 Notice that the broadcast function is exposed. exposed is an Opa keyword that precedes the function keyword. Exposing a function means that we specifically open an endpoint in the server so that clients can call the server-side function register.

If you omit exposed, Opa will have to perform more client/server calls.

Connecting the Model and the View

Now it is time to connect the model and the view.

Connecting the model and the view requires simply calling functions from Model in View. Let's start with a very simple call: author name generation.

In the View module, update the default_page function as follows:

```
function default_page() {
  author = Model.new_author();
  page_template("Opa chat", (chat_html(author)))
}
```

Next, you will learn how to do the following:

- Show new messages as they arrive
- Broadcast the current user's message when it is entered

Showing New Messages

To show new messages, you write a `user_update` function that takes a message as an argument and updates the user interface:

```
function user_update(message msg) {
  line = <div class="row-fluid line">
            <div class="span1 userpic">
              <img src="/resources/img/default-user.jpg" alt="User"/>
            </div>
            <div class="span2 user">{msg.author}:</>
            <div class="span9 message">{msg.text}</>
          </div>;
  #conversation =+ line;
  Dom.scroll_to_bottom(#conversation);
}
```

This code first constructs an HTML representation of the message (`line`) and then prepends this HTML to the DOM element with the `conversation` identifier, using the special syntax `#conversation =+ line` that we discussed in Chapter 5.

Finally, the last command of this function scrolls to the bottom of the `conversation` element to ensure that the most recent messages are visible.

Broadcasting the Current User's Messages

When a user enters a new message, you need to send the message to other users. You can do this with the following function:

```
function broadcast(author) {
  text = Dom.get_value(#entry);
  Model.broadcast(~{author, text});
  Dom.clear_value(#entry);
}
```

Here, the code assigns the content of the user message to `text` by reading the value of the DOM element with the `entry` ID using the `Dom.get_value` function. The second line of this function calls the previously written `Model.broadcast` function of the model to broadcast the message to all chat users. The last line clears the content of the input field, allowing the user to start composing a new chat message.

Connecting Everything

Now that you have all the pieces in place, it is time to connect them. You need to do two things: make sure `broadcast` is invoked whenever a user sends a new message; and make sure `user_udpate` is invoked whenever a new message is sent to the chat room. You will use the event handlers/listeners of the DOM to create connections. Manipulating event handlers should not be difficult at this stage, as you already learned about them in "Event Handlers" (page 43).

You will add all the wiring in the chat_html function. First you need to add an argument to the function author, which is the name of the current user. Then you need to add three event handlers:

- Add the onready event to the conversation element, which is invoked when the page loads and calls the model's register_message_callback function, passing user_update as a callback that should be invoked for every new message received.

- Add the onnewline event to the input box for the user's message, which upon the user pressing the Enter key will call the broadcast function to distribute it to other chat users.

- Add the onclick event to the Post button, which will enable users to send a message by clicking the Post button.

After you make those changes, the function should look like this:

```
function chat_html(author) {
  <div id=#conversation
    onready={function(_) { Model.register_message_callback(user_update)}} />
  <div id=#footer class="navbar navbar-fixed-bottom">
    <div class=container>
      <div class=input-append>
        <input id=#entry class=input-xxlarge type=text
          onnewline={function(_) { broadcast(author) }}>
        <button class="btn btn-primary" type=button
          onclick={function(_) { broadcast(author) }}>Post</>
      </div>
    </div>
  </div>
}
```

You are now ready to compile and run the application. With the *Makefile* generated by opa create, it is as simple as invoking:

```
Tokyo:~ henri$ make run
```

That's it!

Understanding Networks

This advanced section explains the low-level mechanism of networks, which are also accessible in Opa. As we said earlier, networks are based on a lower-level object named sessions. A session in Opa is a unit of state and concurrency:

- Constructing a new session requires you to provide the session's *initial state* and a *message handler*. As a result of constructing a session, a *channel* is created, which provides a means of communicating with the session. A session created on one machine will always remain there; however, its channels can be distributed and duplicated at will.

- When you have access to a session's channel, you can send it a *message*. This message is passed and processed to the message handler. A message handler has access to the current state of the session and, as a result of processing the message, can modify that state.

Let's detail a generic use of sessions, as represented in Figure 6-2.

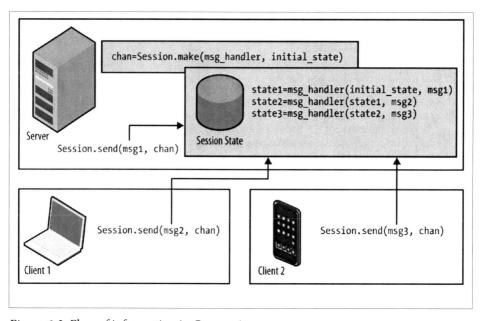

Figure 6-2. Flow of information in Opa sessions

To create a new session, you write:

```
chan = Session.make(msg_handler, initial_state)
```

The resultant value, chan, is a channel that can be used to communicate with the session.

The parameters are initial_state, the value for the initial state of the session, and msg_handler, which is the handler used to process messages sent to this session.

Before we look in detail at what the handler is, note that when chan is created server-side, the session will stay server-side. Reciprocally, if the session is created client-side, it will stay client-side.

The message handler is a function that takes two parameters:

- The current state of the session
- The message that was received

The message responds with a Session.instruction. This has the following type:

```
type Session.instruction('state) = {'state set} or {unchanged} or {stop}
```

The preceding type is a variant of these three types:

- {set: value}, which sets the new value to the state of the session
- {unchanged}, which leaves the state of the session unchanged
- {stop}, which terminates the session; future messages sent to it will be ignored

Let's use this. On a server-side function, you can call:

```
Session.send(msg1, chan)
```

This causes *asynchronous* sending of msg1 to the session identified with chan. Upon receipt of this message, the session will invoke the message handler, in this case resulting in a call to msg_handler(initial_state, msg1).

If the handler responds with {set: state1}, state1 will become the new state of the session.

Later, when the application is executed, a client-side function may then send the following from Client 1:

```
Session.send(msg2, chan)
```

Then it may send the following from another client, Client 2:

```
Session.send(msg3, chan)
```

As a result, "Client 2" will reciprocally invoke msg_handler(state1, msg2) and msg_handler(state2, msg3).

Thanks to Opa's transparent client/server communication, although chan resides server-side, it is OK to pass chan as an argument in the program flow to make it accessible client-side, for instance. It's that simple.

In Opa, you can directly use high-level networks for real-time web applications, but the low-level sessions on which they are built can also be very useful in many more situations.

Exercises

Now it's time to apply what you have learned! Here are a few exercises that will test your Opa skills.

Customizing the Display

Customize the chat app in the following ways:

- Make the text box appear at the top.
- Have each new message added at the top, rather than at the bottom.

You will need to use the += operator instead of =+.

Saying "Hello"

Customize the chat app so that, at startup, in the beginning of #conversation, it displays the following message to the current user: "Hello, you are user 8dh335."

Customize the chat app so that, at startup, it displays the following message to all users: "User 8dh335 has joined the room."

Combine both: customize the chat app so that one user sees something like "Hello, you are user 8dh335" and other users see "User 8dh335 has joined the room."

Distinguishing Messages Between Users

Customize the chat app so that the user's own messages are distinguished from messages sent by other users.

User Customization

Let users choose their own username, and let them choose their own icon. You can let them enter a URI, for instance.

 For security reasons, values with type xhtml cannot be transmitted from one client to another client. So you will have to find another way to send one user's icon to all other users.

And Beyond

And now, here's an open exercise: invent and implement unique features to make your version of the chat app stand out! A starting point here can be a more complete, finished application such as this one (*https://github.com/MLstate/hello_chat*).

CHAPTER 7

More Advanced Features of Opa

Before we dive into developing Birdy, you need to learn few more things about Opa. In this chapter, we will discuss more complex types, which will help you deal with more complex data that you will encounter in this part of the book.

Learning More About Types

You learned about primitive values (`int`, `float`, `string`) in "Primitive Values" (page 13) and about records in "Records" (page 17). Now it is time to extend your type arsenal.

Variant Types

Variant types, as the name suggests, allow you to express values that can take several different variants. Probably the simplest such type is a *boolean* value, which is defined in Opa as follows:

```
type bool = {false} or {true}
```

The variants are separated with the `or` keyword and the variants themselves are just regular record types. Lack of a type for a given field implies it is of type `void` (which we covered in "Event Handlers" (page 43)), so the preceding code can also be written as follows:

```
type bool = {void false} or {void true}
```

Such `void`-typed fields make little sense in regular records, as the field value carries no information. However, in variant types they make perfect sense, as their presence is important and differentiates between variants.

In this simple form, with all variants having just one field of type `void`, those types correspond to *enumeration types*, as you may know from other programming languages. Here is another example from the standard Opa library:

```
type Date.weekday = {monday} or {tuesday} or {wednesday} or {thursday}
    or {friday} or {saturday} or {sunday}
```

However, note that in Opa we are not restricted to such degenerated records. For instance, say we need to keep track of the *logged-in* user, and suppose we have a User.t type describing the user. We can keep track of the logged-in user with the following type:

```
type User.logged = {guest} or {User.t user}
```

Example values of type User.logged are {guest} and {user: u} if u is a value of type User.t. Of course, we are not restricted to single-field records.

Pattern Matching

But how can we work with such values? How do we figure out which variant was used to construct the value; for instance, to check whether the user is logged in?

This is where *pattern matching* comes in handy. Pattern matching is a way of analyzing and decomposing values. At first, it can seem deceptively similar to switch statements, which you may know from languages such as JavaScript, C, and Java, but as you will see later in this chapter, pattern matching can do much more than that.

Let's look at some examples. We'll start with Boolean values:

```
function int int_of_bool(bool b) {
  match (b) {
  case {true}: 1
  case {false}: 0
  }
}
```

Here, the match is followed by an expression (it does not need to be a simple variable) that we want to match against, put in parentheses. This is followed by a number of different matching cases introduced with the case keyword, followed by the matched pattern, a colon, and the expression with the result for that particular case.

Now let's match a value of type User.logged:

```
function string greet(User.logged u) {
  name =
    match (u) {
    case {guest}: "guest"
    case {user: user}: User.get_name(user)
    }
  "Hello, {name}"
}
```

In this second pattern-matching case, user will be matched against the value of the user field in the record u and can be accessed in the expression User.get_name(user). Just as with regular records, you can abbreviate {user: user} to ~{user} in the pattern.

With pattern matching, there are a few things to keep in mind. First, the pattern-matching part of the code is an expression, not a statement (as switch is in many languages). This means it is perfectly permissible to write the previous function as:

```
function string greet(User.logged u) {
   "Hello, " + match (u) {
             case {guest}: "guest"
             case {user: user}: User.get_name(user)
             }
}
```

Second, the compiler makes sure that all possible cases are covered by the given patterns, and otherwise will fail with a *nonexhaustive pattern-matching* error. This means that if at some point you need to add to the program a new feature that requires extending some type with an additional variant, you can safely do so. The compiler will then point out all the places that need to be adjusted because of this change.

Note that in the vocabulary of languages such as Java and C#, pattern-matching combines features of if, switch, instanceof/is, and casting, but without the usual (type) safety issues of the last two operations.

Polymorphic Types

In this section, we will examine at an important extension of variant types: *polymorphism*. We will start with a simple definition:

```
type nullable_int = {null} or {int value}
```

Many programming languages allow a special null value as a value for any type. Not so in Opa. The type in the preceding code describes nullable integers by allowing two types of values: {null} and {value: x} for any integer x.

 Yes, you guessed right: Opa does not have the notorious problem of null pointer exceptions. Using types like the one in the preceding text for situations when you really need "nullability" has one big advantage: while pattern-matching on such values, you will be prompted to explicitly handle the null case.

That seems like a useful definition, but we may need null for values of types other than just int. Repeating it for every single type where we need this feature would be terribly inefficient.

Fortunately, we can do better. Here is a definition from the standard Opa library:

```
type option('a) = {none} or {'a some}
```

Here, `'a` is a *type variable* (type variables always begin with a single apostrophe) and the definition of `option` is parameterized by this type variable. It has two variants: {none}, meaning no value, and {some: x}, representing an existing value x of the parameterized type `'a`.

We call such a type a *polymorphic type* as we can substitute the type variable, `'a`, with an arbitrary type to obtain a concrete type. For instance, you can get optional integers by instantiating `'a` with int to obtain option(int).

Also note that, thanks to Opa's type inference, you will not need to spell out the type names in many cases. If you just write {some: 5}, the compiler will be able to figure out that this is a value of type option(int).

It's important to realize that you can also write *polymorphic functions* like this one:

```
function bool is_some(option('a) v) {
  match (v) {
  case {some: _}: true
  default: false
  }
}
```

The *underscore* in the second pattern means we do not care about this value. It allows us to avoid the *unused variable* warning that would be generated if we used a {some: value} pattern with an unused variable value. It also clearly shows that the value itself is irrelevant. Note that we do not inspect the value, which is why the function can retain a fully generic option('a) type for its v argument and allows us to write:

```
b1 = is_some({some: 5})        // b1 == true
b2 = is_some({some: "Text"})   // b2 == true
b3 = is_some({none})           // b3 == false
```

Another new feature that we used in the previous example is the catchall `default` pattern, which always needs to be specified as the last pattern and handles all the remaining cases.

Note that many functions that handle options are already defined in the standard library; one of these is `Option.default`, which gets the some case and returns the default value of none:

```
Option.default(default_value, option_value)
```

Use `default` sparingly. It is important to use it only when you really want to handle "all remaining cases": a typical use is when you want to distinguish between one particular variant and "everything else."

When not using `default`, the Opa typechecker always ensures that pattern-matching cases are complete. For instance, the following program:

```
option(void) v = none
match (v) {
        case {none}: 1;
}
```

defines an `option` but does not check for the `{some: ...}` case. If you try to compile it, the Opa compiler tells only this:

```
Warning pattern
File "match1.opa", line 2, characters 1-30, (2:1-4:1 | 23-52)
Incomplete pattern matching: case {some} is missing
Error: Fatal warning: 'pattern'
```

The `option` type above has only one type variable, but types with several of them are possible. For instance, here is another type from the standard Opa library:

```
type outcome('ok, 'ko)= { 'ok success } or { 'ko failure }
```

This represents an `outcome` of some operation, which can be either `success`, with the resultant value, or `failure`, with an indication of the problem that occurred. The types of the values returned in case of success and in case of failure can be different. For example, an arithmetic operation could produce an `int` if successful or a `string` indicating the type of problem that occurred. Such an instance would have type `outcome(int, string)`.

Recursive Types

The types you've learned about so far allow you to only express values with a fixed, finite structure. But what about things like lists and trees? This is where recursive types come to the rescue.

A `list` is a finite sequence of values of a given type. In Opa, it is defined as:

```
type list('a) = {nil} or {'a hd, list('a) tl}
```

This is a polymorphic type, with `list('a)` being either an empty list, `{nil}`, or an element `hd` of type `'a` followed by `tl` of type `list('a)`. This definition of a type expressed in terms of itself is what gives it the name *recursive type*.

Traditionally, the first element of a list is called the *head* and the remainder is called the *tail*, hence the field names `hd` and `tl`, respectively.

Opa does not have a type of fixed-size array, and lists are used instead. In fact, lists are used very extensively in Opa, so it is important that you become comfortable with using them.

So how do we represent a list with three elements: 1, 2, and 7?

```
l1 = {hd: 1, tl: {hd: 2, tl: {hd: 7, tl: nil}}}
```

This is not very readable, so Opa supports special syntax for lists that enables us to write the preceding code equivalently as:

```
l2 = [1, 2, 7]
```

Opa also offers [head | tail] syntax for a list with a given head and given tail, so we can write:

```
l3 = [0 | l2]   // == [0, 1, 2, 7]
```

or even:

```
l4 = [0, 3 | l2] // == [0, 3, 1, 2, 7]
```

Recursive types are very useful, so we will conclude this section with an illustration of how to use them to express binary trees (of arbitrary type):

```
type bin_tree('a) = {leaf} or {'a value, tree('a) left, tree('b) right}
```

When writing functions that do pattern matching on recursive types, the functions themselves will often use recursion. Since this is a new and very important concept, we will take a closer look at them in the next section.

Recursive Functions

To pattern-match on recursive types, such as the list introduced in the preceding section, we just follow the same rules we used for records:

```
match (l) {
case {nil}: ...
case ~{hd, tl}: ...
}
```

Here, Opa also offers syntactic sugar, allowing us to replace the preceding code with:

```
match (l) {
case []: ...
case [hd | tl]: ...
}
```

The interesting point here is that the tl binding in the second case will be of the same type as the whole list l. To make this more concrete, let's try to write a function that computes the length of a list:

```
function int length(list('a) l) {
  match (l) {
  case []: 0
  case [hd | tl]: ?
  }
```

The case when the list is empty is easy, as we just return 0 (since that is the length of an empty list). However, how do we handle the second case? What is the length of a list with an element hd followed by a list tl? Well, it is the length of tl plus one (for hd). This is exactly what we can write in Opa, too (we replace hd with an underscore, as we do not need to inspect the head of the list and hence do not need this binding):

```
function int length(list('a) l) {
  match (l) {
  case []: 0
  case [_ | tl]: 1 + length(tl)
  }
```

Note how the length function is called *in the definition* of the length function. This is what makes it a *recursive function*. While writing such functions, we need to be careful, though. What would happen if we just wrote the following?:

```
function f() {
  f()
}
```

Invocation of such a function would cause an infinite loop, just as if we wrote while (true) { } in a language like Java.

One final remark: all *top-level* functions (i.e., functions that are defined in a file or in a module, but *not* local functions that are defined within other functions) can use recursion directly. However, if you want to use recursion in a local function, you will need to precede function with the recursive keyword.

For instance, we can write the following sample functions:

```
function f(x) {
  if (x==1) { 1; }
  else g(x)
}
function g(x) {
  f(x-1)
}

function f(x) {
  recursive function aux(x) {
    if (x==1) { 1; }
    else aux(x-1)
  }
  aux(x)
}
```

What About Loops?

If you're familiar with some programming languages, you may have been wondering why we have not talked about *loops* yet. The reason is simple: there aren't any in Opa.

If you have no prior experience with functional programming, the notion of a lack of loops can be truly confounding; how can you write programs without loops? It turns out that just as you can do without variables [see "Bindings Versus Variables" (page 23)], you can also do without loops.

In Chapter 6, you wrote a function to compute the length of a list using recursion instead of iteration (i.e., loops). It turns out that *recursion* is a very powerful notion and it can replace loops altogether.

Opa has an even more powerful weapon in its arsenal: *iterators*. Iterators in Opa have a slightly different meaning than in imperative languages; they are functions that capture some important schema for manipulating collections.

To make this discussion more concrete, let's discuss three important iterators on lists: `List.filter`, `List.map`, and `List.iter`:

- `List.filter` takes a function `f` and a list `l` and produces a new list containing only those elements of `l` for which `f` returns `true`. In other words, it filters elements of a list based on a given predicate.
- `List.map` takes a function `f` and a list `l` and produces a new list by applying `f` to all elements of `l`. So, if `l = [x1, x2 ,... xN]`, `List.map(f, l) == [f(x1), f(x2), ... f(xN)]`.
- `List.iter` takes a function `f` and a list `l`. It does not produce any result, but it invokes `f` on all elements of `l`. It is equivalent to a `foreach` loop in other languages.

Here is a summary of those iterators:

```
List.map(_ * 3, [1, 2, 3, 4]) = [3, 6, 9, 12]
List.filter(_ < 3, [1, 2, 3, 4]) = [1, 2]
List.iter(f, [1, 2, 3, 4]) = f(1); f(2); f(3); f(4)
```

Now that you've learned about pattern matching, polymorphic types, iterators, recursive types, and functions, it's time to apply this knowledge to a real project.

Bigger Projects

In Coding a Mini Wikipedia of this book, all the applications we developed, except for the chat app, consisted of a single source file. This is fine for very simple projects, but it's unlikely to work very well for more elaborate ones. It is time to learn how to create such projects.

The overhead of creating such projects is minimal, but Opa features a tool that helps in setting up new projects. To get started, change to a root directory in which you can create the new project, and enter the following:

```
Tokyo:opa henri$ opa create birdy --template mvc
```

This will create a new *birdy* directory containing a complete scaffolding for it. The resultant directory is similar to the one in Chapter 6 and has the following structure:

```
+- birdy
| +- Makefile
| +- Makefile.common
| +- opa.conf
| +- resources
| | +- css
| | | +- style.css
| +- src
| | +- model
| | | +- data.opa
| | +- view
| | | +- page.opa
| | +- controller
| | | +- main.opa
```

This newly created project includes the following:

- A *Makefile* file for the project (which can be customized)
- A generic *Makefile.common* file (which usually will not be modified)
- A configuration file, *opa.conf* (which lists all the source files of the project and their dependencies; more about this in a moment)
- An example style file, *style.css*
- The source files, following the classic MVC pattern, divided into three sub-directories: *model*, *view*, and *controller*, for the standard three application layers

The `opa-create` tool allows for some customization; for instance, it supports multiple templates that can be set with the `--template TEMPLATE_NAME` argument. Version 1.1 of Opa supports three templates:

mvc-small (default)
> A template for a small project following the MVC pattern, where the *src* directory contains no subdirectories but only three files: *model.opa*, *view.opa*, and *controller.opa*

mvc
> An MVC template for bigger projects, where the *src* directory contains three folders: *model*, *view*, and *controller*, containing respectively *data.opa*, *page.opa*, and *data.opa*

mvc-wiki

Which is based on *mvc-small* but contains an example wiki application, ready to be modified/extended

Every template provides a *Makefile* that eases the compilation of the project with:

```
make
```

and compilation followed by execution with:

```
make run
```

Your application should look like Figure 7-1.

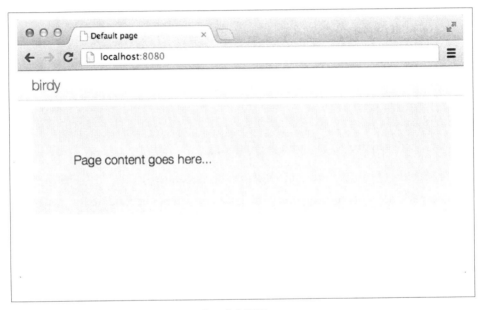

Figure 7-1. Birdy application created with MVC

Let's take a quick look at the *opa.conf* file. In our newly created project, it will look as follows:

```
birdy.controller:
  import birdy.view
  src/controller.opa

birdy.view:
  import birdy.model
  import stdlib.themes.bootstrap
  src/view.opa

birdy.model:
  src/model.opa
```

Usage of such a configuration file is optional, but it can be quite convenient as it creates a central point listing all project files and packages, as well as dependencies between them. You can consider this as a way to sanitize your project further.

Packages

Packages are the main unit of abstraction in Opa. For Birdy, there are three packages: *birdy.controller*, *birdy.view*, and *birdy.model*. Each section starts with optional import statements, followed by the list of paths to files constituting the given package (one file per project in this example).

Packaging is very important in Opa, as typechecking and compilation are done separately at the package level. Packages are therefore highly reusable bits of code and a major addition to JavaScript, which even lacks modules.

Packaging is also very powerful when combined with abstract data types, which hide types from other packages. We will introduce the latter feature in the next chapter.

Summary

In this chapter you learned more about Opa types; in particular, you learned how to use:

- Variant types
- Pattern matching
- Polymorphic types
- Recursive types
- Recursive functions
- Iterators

Using Opa, you generated an MVC template for your first big project, Birdy, looked inside the *opa.conf* file, and learned about packages. In the next chapter you will learn how to manage user accounts in Birdy.

CHAPTER 8

User Management

Managing user accounts is one of the main features of any real application. We would like Birdy users to sign up with their email first, and then be able to sign in.

To create an account, the user will sign up with his email and create his username and password. He will then receive an account activation link via email. After he activates his account, the user will be able to sign in and start posting messages.

Usually, the "Sign in" link for accounts is placed in the top-right corner of the top bar, so that's what we'll do here. We will place the "Sign up" button in the center of the home page. Both links will activate a modal window that contains the login or registration form.

In this chapter you will:

- Create a modal window for registration and learn how to quickly handle Bootstrap components
- Create a registration form and learn how to handle forms
- Create new user accounts
- Send registration code via email and learn how to send emails
- Handle account activation links and learn how to handle data encoded in URLs
- Track a logged-in user throughout the site and learn how to handle user-associated data

Setting Up the View

Before we jump into proper login/registration features, let's take a moment to slightly customize the default view to better suit the needs of our application.

First, take a look at the code of the view part of the application, as it was generated by opa create. You will find it in *src/view/page.opa* and it should look as follows:

```
module Page {

    // View code goes here

    function page_template(title, content) {
      html =
        <div class="navbar navbar-fixed-top">
          <div class=navbar-inner>
            <div class=container>
              <a class=brand href="./index.html">birdy<//>
            </div>
          </div>
        </div>
        <div id=#main class=container-fluid>
          {content}
        </div>
      Resource.page(title, html)
    }

    function default_page() {
      content =
        <div class="hero-unit">
          Page content goes here...
        </div>
      page_template("Default page", content)
    }

}
```

This code defines a Page module with two functions: page_template, which is a template of any page, parameterized by its title and content; and default_page, a default page using the page_template function and which, for now, is set up to be displayed for every page of the application (we will explain this in more detail later).

 To learn more about fixed versus fluid layouts in Bootstrap, as well as many other aspects of the application, visit the project's website (*http:// twitter.github.com/bootstrap*).

Now we will build the Birdy home page using page_template and Bootstrap's hero-unit element. Hero-unit is a clearly visible box for taglines and other important content.

We will put the HTML content of the home page into the main_page_content value:

```
main_page_content =
  <div class=hero-unit>
    <h1>Birdy</h1>
```

```
<h2>Micro-blogging platform.<br/>
    Built with <a href="http://opalang.org">Opa.</a>
  </h2>
</div>
```

We won't use the `default_page` function. Instead, we will create a `main_page` function and use a `page_template` function to display the content:

```
function main_page() {
  page_template("Birdy", main_page_content)
}
```

The last thing to do is to register `main_page` as the default page of the application. This is taken care of by the *controller*, the code of which is in *src/controller/main.opa*. We talked about URL dispatching in "URL Dispatching" (page 31), so the code in that file should not present any surprises and all we have to do for now is replace `Page.default_page` with `Page.main_page`:

```
module Controller {

  // URL dispatcher of your application; add URL handling as needed
  dispatcher = {
    parser {
    case (.*) : Page.main_page()
    }
  }

}
```

After making those changes, run the application and it should look like Figure 8-1.

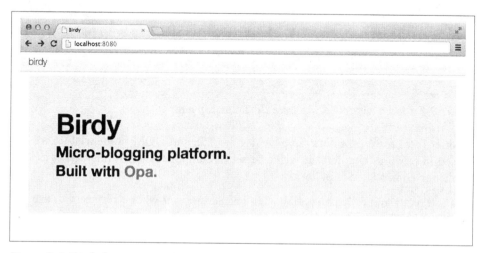

Figure 8-1. Birdy home page v01

Bootstrap Widgets: Modal Windows

We will use Bootstrap to build the modal window UI so that we don't have to deal with graphical widgets manually in Opa: don't reinvent the wheel unless you have to! *Modal windows* are windows that block the main application and require the user to interact with the window before returning control back to it. Figure 8-2 presents a demo of a modal window from the Bootstrap page.

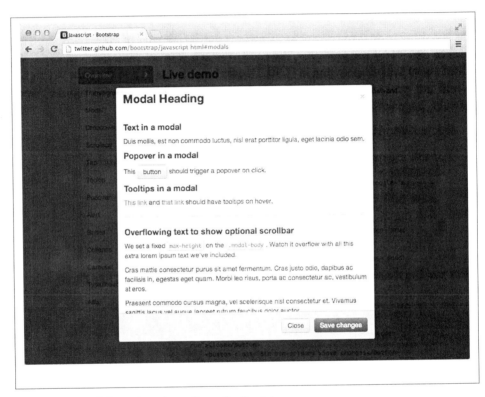

Figure 8-2. Modal window demo from the Bootstrap page

To offer these features, Bootstrap provides the CSS and DOM nomenclature we discussed in previous chapters, as well as a set of components with interaction aspects implemented in a JavaScript library.

Opa is directly and fully compatible with JavaScript, so it will be very easy to use this library and others.

We will start by creating the "Sign up" feature and its user interface. First we'll create a new View file, *src/view/signup.opa*, and add it to the project by modifying the view part of *opa.conf*. Then we'll import the `stdlib.widgets.bootstrap.{modal}` package, which provides the Bootstrap's modal window, drop-down, and alert features in the *opa.conf* file:

```
[...]
birdy.view:
        import birdy.model
    import stdlib.widgets.bootstrap.{modal}
        import stdlib.themes.bootstrap
        src/view/page.opa
    src/view/signup.opa
[...]
```

Note that we are splitting the view into several source files and placing them in a *view* subdirectory.

For now, in the Signup module we would like to have two pieces of the user interface: the modal window and a button to activate it. Since the id attribute of the window will be used to identify it, it is a good practice to make a constant referring to it:

```
module Signup {

    window_id = "signup"

}
```

Now we will create the code for the modal window itself. For this, we will use the Modal.make function of the bootstrap.modal package. It takes five arguments: the window identifier, HTML markup of its header, body, and footer, and the options for the modal window.

```
function modal_window_html() {
  win_body =
    <div>
      Sign up form will appear here
    </>
  win_footer =
    <>
      Submit button will appear here
    </>
  Modal.make(window_id, <>New to Birdy?</>, win_body, win_footer, Modal.
  default_options)
}
```

For now, win_body and win_footer are just placeholders for the registration form and the Submit button that we will put there in "Form Handling in Opa: Registration Form" (page 91).

It is time to create a "Sign up" button on the home page that will fire up the modal window. It will be just a regular HTML link, with the `data-toggle=modal` attribute (which indicates that it's a toggle for the modal window) and the `href` attribute pointing to the ID of the window:

```
signup_btn_html =
  <a class="btn btn-large btn-primary" data-toggle=modal href="#{window_id}">
    Sign up
  </a>
}
```

With those two elements in place, we can put the markup for the modal window, which is invisible by default until window opening is triggered, in `page_template` in *src/view/page.opa*:

```
function page_template(title, content) {
  html =
    <div class="navbar navbar-fixed-top">
      <div class=navbar-inner>
        <div class=container>
          <a class=brand href="./index.html">birdy</>
        </div>
      </div>
    </div>
    <div id=#main class=container-fluid>
      {content}
      {Signup.modal_window_html()}
    </div>
  Resource.page(title, html)
}
```

Here is the code to place the "Sign up" button into `main_page_content`:

```
main_page_content =
  <div class=hero-unit>
    <h1>Birdy</h1>
    <h2>Micro-blogging platform.<br/>
      Built with <a href="http://opalang.org">Opa.</a>
    </h2>
    <p>{Signup.signup_btn_html}</p>
  </div>
```

Our application now looks similar to Figure 8-3, which has some additional style.

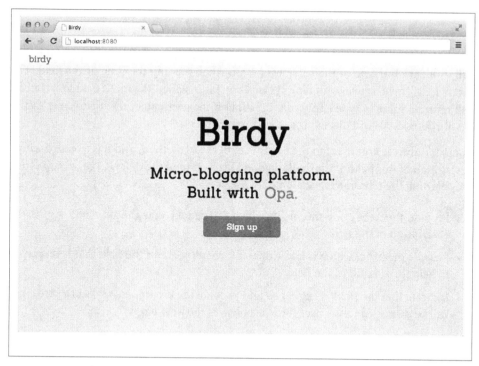

Figure 8-3. Birdy home page v02

Form Handling in Opa: Registration Form

Web forms are used to collect input from the user. Opa makes it very easy to use them by means of the `stdlib.web.forms` package, which we first need to import in the *opa.conf* file:

```
import stdlib.web.forms
```

The two main modules of this package are `Field` and `Form`. The former one is used to create fields of the form and the latter to compose a form of them.

Our registration form will consist of four fields: one each for entering the username, email, password, and a repetition of the password (used to rule out the possibility of making a typo while providing the password). We will turn each field into a private variable in our `Signup` module. For instance, the one for the username field will look as follows:

```
private fld_username =
  Field.text_field({Field.new with
    label: "Username",
    required: {with_msg: <>Please enter your username.</>},
```

```
    hint: <>Username is publicly visible. You will use it to sign in.</>
})
```

We used the `Field.text_field` function to create a new text field. The type of the field will influence the type of the value we obtain when reading the state of the field. The text field will give us a value of type `string`, but, for instance, the input field for an email will return a value of type `Email.email`. What if the user enters text that is not a valid email address? We will discuss that topic in a moment.

There is only one argument to the `Field.text_field` method, and it is a record with a description of this field. It is usually a good idea to extend the default `Field.new` value, only alerting the relevant aspects. In our case, we:

- Provide the `label` for this field, which is the text that the user will see as the description of the field
- Provide the `hint`, which is additional information about the field that is displayed to help the user fill in the field
- Indicate that the field is `required` and provide the error message (`with_msg`) that will be displayed to the user if the user leaves the field empty

In a similar manner, we can create a field for the user's email, but now using the `Field.email_field` function:

```
private fld_email =
  Field.email_field({Field.new with
    label: "Email",
    required: {with_msg: <>Please enter a valid email address.</>},
    hint: <>Your activation link will be sent to this address.</>
  })
```

Next in line is the field for the password:

```
private fld_passwd =
  Field.passwd_field({Field.new with
    label: "Password",
    required: {with_msg: <>Please enter your password.</>},
    hint: <>Password should be at least 6 characters long and contain at least
one digit.</>,
    validator: {passwd: Field.default_passwd_validator}
  })
```

We use the `Field.passwd_field` which also creates a field with an associated value of type `string`, but the field shows asterisks instead of the actual text to protect the password from onlookers, and the obtained string value is a *hashed* value of the password, ready to be stored in the database. Storing plain-text passwords is unacceptable from the point of view of security, and this feature of Opa form management enforces the good practice of properly processing the password before storing it. Whenever a web application or service is able to send you an email that contains your password in clear text (e.g., when you've forgotten it), you know you are in trouble!

The only other new aspect is the validator, which is a `passwd` validator for password, and is parameterized by the specification of the site's requirements on the passwords that can be used by its users. In this case, we are happy with the default specification of `Field.default_passwd_validator`, which corresponds to the requirements that are outlined in the `hint`.

Finally, our last field is the repeated password:

```
private fld_passwd2 =
  Field.passwd_field({Field.new with
    label: "Repeat password",
    required: {with_msg: <>Please repeat your password.</>},
    validator: {equals: fld_passwd, err_msg: <>Your passwords do not match.</>}
  })
```

The only new piece here is the `equals` validator that checks that a value of the field is precisely the same as the previous one, `fld_passwd` here. The beauty of Opa's type safety is also visible here: we can only enforce equality for two fields of the same type. If we tried to ensure equality of, for example, one field with an email and another one with a password, we would end up with a compile type error message.

Now that we have all the fields in place, we can construct a form with those fields and put it in place of the previous placeholder in our modal window. The new version of the `modal_window_html` function becomes:

```
function modal_window_html() {
    form = Form.make(signup, {})
    fld = Field.render(form, _)
    form_body =
      <>
        {fld(fld_username)}
        {fld(fld_email)}
        {fld(fld_passwd)}
        {fld(fld_passwd2)}
      </>
    win_body = Form.render(form, form_body)
    win_footer =
      <a href="#" class="btn btn-primary btn-large" onclick={Form.submit_
      action(form)}>Sign up</>
    Modal.make(window_id, <>New to Birdy?</>, win_body, win_footer, Modal.
    default_options)
}
```

Let's go through this code step by step. First, we create a new empty form by calling the `Form.make` function. It takes two arguments: a function to call on successful form submission (`signup`, which we will write next) and a configuration record, which allows a certain degree of customization for the form. Here we are happy with the defaults, and therefore just supply it with an empty record.

Second, we construct `form_body`, which is just a regular `xhtml` value. We place form fields there with calls to the `Field.render` function, which takes two arguments: the form and its field to render. Since we will be repeatedly displaying fields of a single form, we first create a convenient abbreviation, `fld`, and use it subsequently to construct the `form_body` value.

Then, we replace the previous placeholder that we used for the window body (`win_body`) with the form, which we get using the `Form.render` function with two arguments: the form and its body.

Finally, we add a "Sign up" button. Its `onclick` event invokes the `Form.submit_action` function, which takes care of form processing by doing the following:

- It validates all form fields and informs the user if there are any errors.
- If the form validation is successful, it calls the function responsible for form processing, which was provided in the `Form.make` function (`signup` in our case). We will discuss this in more detail.

It is worth noting that Opa takes care of all the form handling for us, including (client-side) form validation, presentation of error messages, and presentation of explanatory text to the user (optionally, only for the active field), among other features.

Now it is time to focus on the missing `signup` function, which is called when the form validates successfully:

```
private client function signup(_) {
  email = Field.get_value(fld_email) ? error("Cannot read form email")
  username = Field.get_value(fld_username) ? error("Cannot read form name")
  passwd = Field.get_value(fld_passwd) ? error("Cannot read form passwd")
  Modal.hide(#{window_id})
  new_user = ~{email, username, passwd}
  #notice =
    match (User.register(new_user)) {
      case {success: _}:
        Page.alert("Congratulations! You are successfully registered. You will
receive an email with account activation instructions shortly.", "success")
      case {failure: msg}:
        Page.alert("Your registration failed: {msg}", "error")
    }
}
```

First, we read the values of the three form fields using the `Field.get_value` function. The fourth, repeated password, being redundant, is skipped. On the next line we hide the modal window, with `Modal.hide`. Then we construct a record, `new_user`, holding all user-provided information, and call a function to register this new user, `User.`

`register`, which we will build in "Modeling and Adding Users" (page 96). This function will return a value of type `outcome(void, string)`. Depending on this outcome, we construct an appropriate alert message and put its content in the element with the `notice` ID, which will be used for system messages and which we will pass to the function `page_template`:

```
<span id=#notice class=container>{notice}</span>

    ...
    <div id=#main class=container>
      <span id=#notice />
      {content}
    </>
    ...
```

Alerts

Let's discuss `Page.alert` now. As you can see, this function contains two parameters: the first represents the text message that will be displayed, and the second corresponds to the class of the Bootstrap alert box.

Bootstrap has several styles for alert messages: we will use the classes `.error` and `.success`. The HTML structure of all alerts is the same, but we will need to change the class and message for each alert.

Let's add `alert` to the `import stdlib.widgets.bootstrap` package of the configuration file:

```
[...]
birdy.view:
  import birdy.model
  import stdlib.widgets.bootstrap.{modal,alert}
[...]
```

Now we'll create an `alert` function in *src/view/page.opa* that will take those two parameters:

```
function alert(message, cl) {
    <div class="alert alert-{cl}">
      <button type="button" class="close" data-dismiss="alert">×</button>
      {message}
    </div>
}
```

We also need to add `notice` as a third argument to our `page_template` function. Then, we will display the alert message inside the HTML element, `#notice div`.

```
function page_template(title, content, notice) {
    html =
      <div class="navbar navbar-fixed-top">
        ...
```

```
        </div>
        <div id=#main class=container-fluid>
          <span id=#notice class=container>{notice}</span>
          {content}
          {Signup.modal_window_html()}
        </div>
      Resource.page(title, html)
    }
```

Finally, we should also update the `main_page` function:

```
function main_page() {
    page_template("Birdy", main_page_content, <></>)
  }
```

Modeling and Adding Users

So far you've learned about the *view* part of the registration process, so now it is time to turn our attention to the *model*.

We will need to create two new files:

- *src/model/user.opa*, which will contain a `User` module representing a user of our application

- *src/model/topic.opa*, for the `Topic` module

Let's add them to the *src/model/opa.conf* file:

```
[...]
birdy.model:
        src/model/data.opa
        src/model/user.opa
        src/model/topic.opa
```

Before we start working on model files, let's learn some type definitions.

 Type definitions can only be given at the top level, outside of all modules. However, it is customary to use the same prefix; for instance, to use the `User.xxx` pattern for all type definitions related to the `User` module. We will follow this convention.

Let's start with a type definition for the username:

```
abstract type User.name = string
```

This is an *abstract* type. This means the type can be treated as a string *within* the package in which this type declaration occurs; however, *outside* of this package it is opaque, and therefore can only be manipulated by functions from the package. This is a very powerful abstraction mechanism that allows you to hide implementation details and expose only those operations on values of a given type that you choose to expose. It also helps tremendously in terms of making sure that value invariants are preserved, as we will discuss soon.

Then we introduce the user's status:

```
abstract type User.status = {active} or {string activation_code}
```

The user account can be either active or awaiting activation, in which case we store the activation_code.

We then declare a type for topics in */src/model/topic.opa*:

```
abstract type Topic.t = string
```

This is just a synonym for a string, but by making it abstract we make sure that it is opaque and can only be manipulated within the package.

We are now ready to give a definition of the user's account in the *src/model/user.opa* file:

```
abstract type User.info =
  { Email.email email,
    string username,
    string passwd,
    User.status status,
    list(User.name) follows_users,
    list(Topic.t) follows_topics
  }
```

This definition consists of the user's email, username, password (passwd), status, a list of people the user is following (follows_users), and the list of topics the user follows (follows_topics, a feature that is sadly missing in the Twitter service).

With those declarations in place, we will provide the following database definition, consisting of a set of users indexed by their usernames in *src/model/data.opa*:

```
database birdy {
  User.info /users[{username}]
}
```

You can choose to have many separate database declarations in modules to which they relate, or one central declaration in a dedicated place. For Birdy, we chose the latter approach.

Now we are ready to write our User.register function in *src/model/user.opa*:

```
exposed function outcome register(user) {
  activation_code = Random.string(15)
  user =
    { email: user.email,
      username: user.username,
```

```
        passwd: user.passwd,
        follows_users: [],
        follows_topics: [],
        status:{~activation_code}
    }
    x = ?/birdy/users[{username: user.username}]
    match (x) {
      case {none}:
        /birdy/users[{username: user.username}] <- user
            send_registration_email({~activation_code, username:user.username,
email: user.email})
        {success}
      case {some: _}:
        {failure: "User with the given name already exists."}
    }
  }
```

Let's digest the code step by step. First, we randomly generate the `activation_code` for the new user. The `Random.string` function constructs a string of a given length consisting exclusively of lowercase letters. A more generic `Random.generic_string` function is also available, which takes a string s and a number n and constructs a random string of length n consisting of characters present in s.

Next, we construct a value, `user`, that represents a new user (it will be of type `User.info`). Finally, we query the database and check whether a user with the given name already exists. If that is the case, we return `failure`, indicating that the username is already taken. Otherwise, we add this value to the database, invoke `send_registra tion_email` (we will work on that next), and indicate `success`.

Account Creation Notification: Sending Emails

The next step is to send an email to the user, in order to verify that her email address is correct. The email will contain a link with the randomly generated activation code. By clicking on it, the user will complete account activation.

First we will import two packages, `stdlib.web.mail` and `stdlib.web.mail.smtp. client`, into the *model* part of the configuration file. The former is a generic package for email-related activities and the latter is the client for the SMTP, the protocol used for sending emails.

```
birdy.model:
    import stdlib.web.mail
    import stdlib.web.mail.smtp.client
    src/model/data.opa
    src/model/user.opa
[...]
```

At the same time, we'll update the *view* part by adding the `import stdlib.web.client` package:

```
birdy.view:
[...]
    import stdlib.web.client
```

The `stdlib.web.mail` package contains, among other things, these two type definitions:

```
type Email.content = {string text} or {xhtml html} or {string text, xhtml html}

type Email.send_status = { void bad_sender } or { void bad_recipient } or
{ void sending } or { string ok } or { string error }
```

The `stdlib.web.mail.smtp.client` contains, among other things, two functions for sending email:

```
Email.send_status try_send (Email.email from, Email.email to, string subject,
Email.content content, Email.options options)

void try_send_async (Email.email from, Email.email to, string subject,
Email.content content, Email.options options, (Email.send_status → void)
continuation)
```

The `Email.content` type defines the content of the email, allowing the user to provide only a text version, only an HTML version, or both. Then the first five arguments of both functions are the same and include the email address of the sender (`from`) and recipient (`to`), the email `subject`, the email `content`, and sending `options`.

 Most modern email clients accept rich HTML emails, but some accept only plain-text messages. Therefore, most email messages contain both versions of the content. If you provide only the HTML content of the message to Opa's email sending functions, the plain-text version will be automatically generated from it.

The `try_send` function sends the email *synchronously*, returning the status of the operation. The `try_send_async` function sends it *asynchronously*, and once the sending is complete, it invokes the `continuation` function with the status of the operation.

Now let's write the missing `send_registration_email` function, where we use the asynchronous method of sending emails and ignore the status:

```
private function send_registration_email(args) {
  from = Email.of_string("no-reply@{Data.main_host}")
  subject = "Birdy says welcome"
  email =
      <p>Hello {args.username}!</p>
      <p>Thank you for registering with Birdy.</p>
```

```
        <p>Activate your account by clicking on
          <a href="http://{Data.main_host}{Data.main_port}/activation/{args.
          activation_code}">
            this link
          </a>.
        </p>
        <p>Happy messaging!</p>
        <p>--------------</p>
        <p>The Birdy Team</p>
    content = {html: email}
    continuation = function(_) { void }
    SmtpClient.try_send_async(from, args.email, subject, content, Email.
    default_options, continuation)
}
```

The email contains an *activation link* that consists of the name of the domain at which the application is deployed (which is parameterized as a constant), followed by the /activation/ path and then the sequence of characters constituting the activation code itself.

If we deploy our application on the example.com domain, the Data module should contain a constant declaration:

```
module Data {
    main_host = "example.com"
}
```

An example activation link would be:

```
http://example.com/activation/swxrjvaprz
```

To be able to test emails deploying the application locally, we will declare main_host and main_port separately:

```
module Data {
    main_host = "localhost"
    main_port = ":8080"
}
```

As you can see, sending emails does not differ much from constructing regular web pages (although clearly you should refrain from using event handlers in email messages), allowing code reuse between those two features.

Now you can run the application and test the sign-up form. It should look similar to Figure 8-4, which has some additional styling.

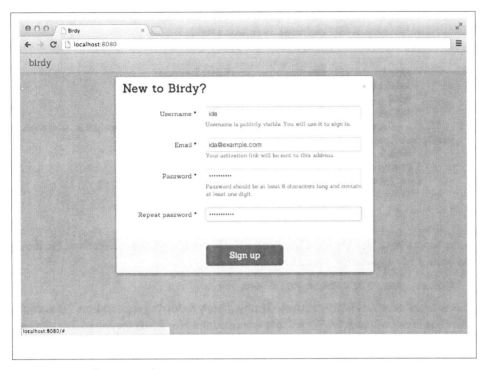

Figure 8-4. Birdy sign-up form

Activating a User Account Without an Activation Email

Before we more forward, we would like to show you how to add an option to be able to test the application locally without sending users' activation links via email.

We have to modify our user `register` function and add an additional user status of `NO_ACTIVATION_MAIL`, which should be set to `active` like so:

```
exposed function outcome register(user) {
    activation_code = Random.string(15)
    status =
      #<Ifstatic:NO_ACTIVATION_MAIL>
      {active}
      #<Else>
      {~activation_code}
      #<End>
    user =
      { email: user.email,
        username: user.username,
        passwd: user.passwd,
        follows_users: [],
        follows_topics: [],
        ~status
```

```
      }
    x = ?/birdy/users[{username: user.username}]
    match (x) {
      case {none}:
        /birdy/users[{username: user.username}] <- user
        #<Ifstatic:NO_ACTIVATION_MAIL>
        void
        #<Else>
              send_registration_email({~activation_code, username:user.username,
email: user.email})
        #<End>
        {success}
      case {some: _}:
        {failure: "User with the given name already exists."}
    }
  }
```

In the function <Ifstatic> , <Else> and #<End> are compilation directives. So, if you
run your Birdy application using this command:

```
Moorea:~ ida$ NO_ACTIVATION_MAIL=1 make run
```

all new users' accounts will be activated immediately following registration. No account
activation email will be sent. We will use this command for Birdy testing so that we don't
need to set a domain name.

Account Activation: URL Data Handling

The last thing we need to do to complete the registration process is to handle user
account activation.

We need to handle URLs of the form /activation/ACTIVATION_CODE that we generated
previously. This is the role of the *controller*. First, let's change its style, from parsing
against an unstructured string to matching against a structured representation of a URL,
as we discussed in "URL Dispatching" (page 31).

To do that, we first replace { custom: Controller.dispatcher } with {dispatch:
Controller.dispatcher } in the server definition in *src/controller/main.opa*. Then we
need to change the definition of the Controller.dispatch function accordingly. The
new version will look as follows:

```
function dispatcher(Uri.relative url) {
  match (url) {
  case {path: ["activation", activation_code] ...}:
    Signup.activate_user(activation_code)
  default:
    Page.main_page()
  }
}
```

We've included two cases here. The first one handles URLs following the pattern /activation/ACTIVATION_CODE and dispatches rendering of those requests to Signup.activate_user, with the given ACTIVATION_CODE as the only function argument. The second one is a catchall case that dispatches all other requests to the main page that we developed previously.

That was the controller part. Now let's change the view part. We need to add the function activate_user to our Signup module:

```
function activate_user(activation_code) {
  notice =
    match (User.activate_account(activation_code)) {
    case {success: _}:
      Page.alert("Your account is activated now.", "success") <+>
      <div class="hero-unit">
        <div class="well form-wrap">
          {Signin.form()}
        </div>
      </div>
    case {failure: _}:
      Page.alert("Activation code is invalid.", "error") <+>
      Page.main_page_content
    }
  Page.page_template("Account activation", <></>, notice)
}
```

This produces a page using Page.page_template. The content depends on the result of the call to the model function User.activate_account, which tries to activate the user account with the given activation code. Depending on whether that is successful or not, we display to the user an appropriate notification message placing it inside the notice element.

Finally, let's set the model part and the User.activate_account function:

```
exposed function outcome activate_account(activation_code) {
  user = /birdy/users[status == ~{activation_code}]
      |> DbSet.iterator
      |> Iter.to_list
      |> List.head_opt
  match (user) {
  case {none}: {failure}
  case {some: user}:
    /birdy/users[{username: user.username}] <- {user with status: {active}}
    {success}
  }
}
```

Note that we use *pipes* here. A pipe, |>, takes the result and sends it to the following function.

First, we search for all accounts whose status is inactive and whose activation code corresponds to the one given as a parameter to this function. That gives us a database set, which we then convert to a list and try to get its head.

If there is no head in the list, this means no user account is pending with the given activation code, so we respond with a `{failure}` result. Otherwise, we have the corresponding user and we just update his status to `{active}` and return `{success}`, in which case he will see the notification message saying that activation was successful. Now the user can sign in, so it is time to develop the login feature for our application.

Keeping Track of Logged-In User: Handling User Associated Data

How do we keep track of information related to the currently connected user?

Before we answer that question, let's begin with two user-related type definitions, in the *src/model/user.opa* file:

```
type User.t = { Email.email email, User.name username }
```

Values of type `User.info` contain all the information about the user, including his (hashed) password. Therefore, we should be careful with passing those values to the client side, as that would be inefficient: most of this data is not needed most of the time, and moreover, the values contain sensitive information.

A typical approach in such a situation is to create a simplified type containing a subset of the data and use it in most of the places. This is the role of the `User.t` definition. For more complex types, it often makes sense to create simplified "views" on a type, as one of the fields. In our case, that would mean:

```
type User.t = { Email.email email, User.name username }
abstract type User.info =
  { User.t data,
    string passwd,
    User.status status,
    list(User.name) follows_users,
    list(Topic.t) follows_topics
  }
```

But for our application, we will stick with the previous definitions instead.

We can now introduce a type to store information about the currently logged-in user:

```
type User.logged = {guest} or {User.t user}
```

You can see that this type is functionally equivalent to `option(User.t)`, as it essentially stores an optional value of type `User.t`. But having such dedicated descriptive types often leads to much cleaner code and easier understanding of the code.

So now we are ready to answer the question we posed earlier: how do we associate data with the currently connected user? In Opa, this is achieved with the `UserContext` module:

```
private UserContext.t(User.logged) logged_user = UserContext.make({guest})
```

The `UserContext.make` function creates a new user-aware value, and the argument given to it is the initial value for every user. We can then read it with the `UserContext.get` function or modify it with `UserContext.set`, in which case it will only be modified for the relevant user.

 Association of `UserContext` values with users is short-lived and does not survive a server restart or cookie-cleaning operation. All values that need to be persisted in a longer context should be stored in the database.

To get `username` and `email` out of `User.info`, we will use the following function:

```
private function User.t mk_view(User.info info) {
  {username: info.username, email: info.email}
}
```

We can now write the login function:

```
exposed function outcome(User.t, string) login(username, passwd) {
  x = ?/birdy/users[~{username}]
  match (x) {
  case {none}: {failure: "This user does not exist."}
  case {some: user}:
    match (user.status) {
    case {activation_code: _}:
      {failure: "You need to activate your account by clicking the link we sent
you by email."}
    case {active}:
      if (user.passwd == passwd) {
        user_view = mk_view(user)
        UserContext.set(logged_user, {user: user_view})
        {success: user_view}
      } else
        {failure: "Incorrect password. Try again."}
    }
  }
}
```

We query the database for a user with the given username, and if it is absent, we fail with the "This user does not exist." message. Otherwise, we check the user's status. If it's awaiting activation, we fail with the appropriate message. Finally, we compare the user's password with the given one. If they match, we use `UserContext.set` to note that the user is now logged in, and we succeed with the value representing the user; otherwise, we fail with "Incorrect password…"

We can now turn our attention to the *view* layer. Let's create a new file, *src/view/signin.opa*, with a new `Signin` module and add it to the configuration file.

We begin by constructing the login form; first, we create its fields:

```
window_id = "signin"

  private fld_username =
    Field.text_field({Field.new with
      label: "Username",
      required: {with_msg: <>Please enter your username.</>}
    })

  private fld_passwd =
    Field.passwd_field({Field.new with
      label: "Password",
      required: {with_msg: <>Please enter your password.</>}
    })
```

No surprises here: just two fields for the username and password, and we saw them both in the sign-up form. Now let's build the form itself:

```
  private function register(_) {
    Modal.hide(#{window_id});
    Modal.show(#{Signup.window_id});
  }

  function modal_window_html() {
    form = Form.make(signin(none, _), {})
    fld = Field.render(form, _)
    form_body =
      <>
        {fld(fld_username)}
        {fld(fld_passwd)}
        <div id=#signin_result />
        <div class="control-group">
          <div class="controls">New to Birdy? <a onclick={register}>Sign up</>.
          </div>
        </div>
      </>
    win_body = Form.render(form, form_body)
    win_footer =
      <a href="#" class="btn btn-primary btn-large" onclick={Form.submit_
      action(form)}>Sign in</>
    Modal.make(window_id, <>Sign in</>, win_body, win_footer, Modal.default_
    options)
  }
```

This code is very similar to its sign-up counterpart. Perhaps the only novel part is that the form body, apart from the two fields, contains a link allowing a user without an account to sign up. The `onclick` action of this link simply closes the sign-in modal window and opens the one for signing up.

To handle the sign-up action, we will call `modal_window_html` in `page_template` in *src/view/page.opa*:

```
function page_template(title, content) {
  [...]
    <div id=#main class=container-fluid>
      {content}
      {Signin.modal_window_html()}
      {Signup.modal_window_html()}
    </div>
  [...]
}
```

For a better user experience, we will add the following function that displays the "Sign in" form on the page where the user is redirected after successful account activation:

```
function form() {
  form = Form.make(signin(some("/"), _), {})
  fld = Field.render(form, _)
  form_body =
    <div class="signin_form">
      <legend>Sign in and start messaging</legend>
      {fld(fld_username)}
      {fld(fld_passwd)}
      <a href="#" class="btn btn-primary btn-large"
         onclick={Form.submit_action(form)}>Sign in</>
    </div>
  Form.render(form, form_body)
}
```

The last bit is the `signin` function to be called to process the form:

```
private function signin(redirect, _) {
    username = Field.get_value(fld_username) ? error("Cannot get login")
    passwd = Field.get_value(fld_passwd) ? error("Cannot get passwd")
    match (User.login(username, passwd)) {
    case {failure: msg}:
      #signin_result =
        <div class="alert alert-error">
          {msg}
        </div>
      Dom.transition(#signin_result, Dom.Effect.sequence([
        Dom.Effect.with_duration({immediate}, Dom.Effect.hide()),
        Dom.Effect.with_duration({slow}, Dom.Effect.fade_in())
      ])) |> ignore
    case {success: _}:
      match (redirect) {
      case {none}: Client.reload()
      case {some:url}: Client.goto(url)
      }
    }
  }
```

Here we fetch the values of the form fields and invoke the model's `User.login` function. In case of failure, we put an error message in the `signin_result` placeholder and then perform a simple animation to fade in this message. In case of success, we redirect the user to her wall page, the `/user/USERNAME` URL, which will contain the user's own messages, messages posted by users she follows, and messages mentioning topics she follows; a first-time user will land on an empty page where she can start posting messages. We will develop this later in "User and Topic Pages" (page 142).

We need to add an accessory function in the `User` module for the username exposed as a string (remember that the `User.name` type is abstract):

```
function string get_name(User.t user) {
  user.username
}
```

The User's Top-Bar Menu

As we decided in the beginning of the application development process, the "Sign in" link should be placed on the top bar of the page. To do this, we will create a contextual element that displays a "Sign in" link for users who have not yet logged in, and a drop-down menu with a link to log out (or other features) for logged-in users.

We will need to know who is logged in and be able to log them out, so let's start by adding two appropriate functions in our `User` module:

```
function User.logged get_logged_user() {
  UserContext.get(logged_user)
}

function logout() {
  UserContext.set(logged_user, {guest})
}
```

Since we will be using a drop-down menu, let's add `dropdown` to the `import stdlib.widgets.bootstrap` package of the configuration file, create a new *src/view/topbar.opa* file with a `Topbar` module in the `birdy.view` package, and add it to the configuration file as well.

In our `Page` module, we will move the top-bar markup to this newly created `Topbar` module, so we replace this:

```
...
  <div class=container>
    <a class=brand href="./index.html">birdy</>
  </div>
...
```

with this:

```
...
  <div class=container>
    {Topbar.html()}
  </>
...
```

Now we will add the HTML elements taken from the Page module to the Topbar module. We will also create a user_menu element.

```
function html() {
  <a class=brand href="/">
    Birdy
  </a> <+>
  user_menu()
}
```

Now let's use the Bootstrap nav element to style the "Sign in" link and the drop-down menu:

```
signinup_btn_html =
  <ul class="nav pull-right">
    <li>
      <a data-toggle=modal href="#{Signin.window_id}">Sign in</a>
    </li>
  </ul>

function user_menu() {
  match (User.get_logged_user()) {
    case {guest}: signinup_btn_html
    case ~{user}: user_box(user.username)
  }
}
```

The user_menu function checks whether the user is currently logged in. If the user is logged in, we add the user_box to the top bar; if not, we include a reference to the "Sign in" link.

```
private function user_box(username) {
  id = Dom.fresh_id()
  <ul id={id} class="nav pull-right">
    <li class="dropdown">
      <a href="#" class="dropdown-toggle" data-toggle="dropdown">
        {username}
        <b class="caret"></b>
      </a>
      <ul class=dropdown-menu>
        <li><a onclick={logout} href="#">Sign out<//></>
      </>
    </>
  </>
}
```

The user_box function first obtains a unique DOM ID for the drop-down menu. Thus far, we have always used manually chosen identifiers, which is fine for fixed elements, and therefore, we could have used them here as well. However, if we generate DOM elements programmatically, we may need some other way of assigning identifiers to them. This is the role of Dom.fresh_id.

Once again we will use the Bootstrap nav element to style our username link and a dropdown menu. We create a <ul> element with appropriate markup for a Bootstrap drop-down menu. Use of the data-toggle attribute with Bootstrap allows us to activate the menu by clicking on the username link. The drop-down menu items are encoded via the <ul> tag. For now we only have a single entry for Sign out, which calls the logout function when the user logs out:

```
private function logout(_) {
  User.logout();
  Client.reload()
}
```

The logout function logs the user out and reloads the page, via Client.reload, to refresh the top bar; our element will now indicate that no user is logged in.

Compile and run your Birdy application now to test the "Sign in" form, which should look similar to Figure 8-5.

Figure 8-5. Birdy "Sign in" form

Exercise

The activation mechanism provided in the application is pretty simple. In particular, nothing prevents conflicts between the activation of different users. Can you fix that?

Summary

In this chapter you learned how to:

- Build user registration and user login forms using modals
- Send user registration emails
- Handle user account activation
- Track logged-in users
- Manage URLs and more

CHAPTER 9

Building Reactive UIs: New Messages with a Real-Time Preview

We will now work on a modal window to post new messages in Birdy. As in the micro-blogging app developed earlier, we want certain markup to be interpreted in a special way. More precisely:

- `#topic` text should indicate messages about a given topic.
- `@user` should indicate that the message is directed to the given user.
- *http://example.com-like* text should be interpreted as links.

Those three elements will be formatted in a special way. This formatting will be shown to the user in a *live preview*, which is a preview of the final rendering of the message updated with every keystroke. A UI in which the interface reacts continuously to user events is called a *reactive UI*.

Let's get started!

Parsing

To analyze all the special elements in our messages, we will need to *parse* them. Parsing is the process of analyzing text to determine its structure. The code that performs such an analysis is called a *parser*. Opa offers extensive support for building parsers, so let's begin by exploring this support.

A popular set of rules for parsing goes by the name *context-free grammar* (CFG). Opa does not use CFG, and instead uses a newer set of rules known as *parsing expression grammar* (PEG). You do not need prior knowledge of these rules to understand the concepts presented in this chapter. We just wanted you to know about them!

Parsing is somewhat similar to pattern matching. Pattern matching analyzes an arbitrary *data structure* and computes some value depending on the result of this analysis. Parsing is a similar process, only the input is a *string*. In Opa, parsing can also be applied to one of the foundation data types of web apps: XML. Therefore, parsing in Opa is a way to compute a result depending on the value of a string or an XML fragment; but this book only covers parsing of strings.

The code that performs parsing is called a parser. Opa offers extensive support for building parsers, so let's begin by exploring it. Opa parsers are introduced with the `parser` keyword followed by a number of cases. Each case follows this scheme:

```
case EXPR: VALUE
```

This consists of the `case` keyword (just like in pattern matching) and then a parsing expression (more on that shortly) and the value corresponding to the given case (again, just like in pattern matching). Cases are evaluated one by one, in order. Similar to pattern matching, the first succesful `VALUE` is used. Note that `VALUE`s in all parser cases must be of the same type `t`, and then the type of the complete parser expression is `Parser.general_parser(t)`.

Now let's explore the parsing expressions. The simplest one is just an explicit literal string where the parsed string contains the given text. Hence, the simplest parser one can write is:

```
simple_parser =
  parser {
    case "Hello Opa": {success}
  }
```

This has only one `case`, which expects the precise `Hello Opa` text. It has type `Parser.general_parser({success})`. The main function that uses such parsers is:

```
Parser.try_parse(parser, text)
```

This function takes two arguments: the first one is the parser to be used and the second one is the text (`string`) to parse. The result is `option(t)` if `parser` was of type `Parser.general_parser(t)`, i.e., it is an optional value of the type produced by the parser.

For example, we will have the following two results:

```
Parser.try_parse(simple_parser, "Hello Opa") == some({success})
Parser.try_parse(simple_parser, "Hello") == none
```

Parsing Expressions

Let's continue to extend our arsenal of parsing expressions. A set of collating elements between square brackets is a *range expression*, which parses a single provided character if it belongs to the given set. It also allows ranges using a hyphen (-); for example, [a-zA-Z_] is an expression that accepts a letter (lowercase or uppercase) or an underscore character.

Next in line is the *sequence expression*. If E1 and E2 are parsing expressions, E1 E2 is a parsing expression that means "parse E1 and then E2".

On to the *repetition expression*. If E is a parsing expression, E+ and E* are valid expressions, the former denoting one or more occurrences of E and the latter denoting zero or more occurrences of E. Note that as many occurrences as possible are consumed from the input. Hence, the parsing expression [ab]* [a] will never succeed: [ab]* will consume all as from the input and there will be none left for the final [a] to match against. We say that the repetition operator of PEG is *greedy*, meaning it consumes as much as it can from the input.

CFG is different from PEG in two main ways:

- PEG is greedy: it consumes as much input as possible.
- The choice operator in PEG is prioritized: if a certain case expression succeeds, other ones will never be tried.

Both properties make writing PEG easier, as their behavior is more easily predictable than in CFG.

We are now ready to write a parser for an arbitrary word consisting of a sequence of letters, digits, underscores, and hyphen characters:

```
word = parser { case word=([a-zA-Z0-9_\-]+) -> Text.to_string(word) }
```

Here we have escaped the hyphen in the range operator, as it's meant as a hyphen operator and not part of a range, like in [a-z].

Second, as you saw earlier, every expression has a default parsing value associated with it. For instance, the range operator gives the character that was parsed and the repetition operators give a list of values of parsed elements. So the [a-zA-Z0-9_\-]+ expression would give us a list of parsed characters. Since we're not interested in individual characters, but rather in the complete parsed text, we put the expression in parentheses, which has precisely this effect: the result of parsing (E) is always the text that was consumed while parsing E.

Finally, for efficiency, parsing uses a special data type of text, which is better suited for complex text manipulation than the default string type. It's easy to convert from text to the more classic string using the Text.to_string function, which is part of the standard Opa library.

With all this knowledge at hand, we can turn to our original task: parsing Birdy messages. This task essentially consists of extracting three types of elements from the message: user mentions (@user), topic mentions (#topic), and links (*http://example.com*). Here is a parser that recognizes those elements:

```
element = parser {
    case "@" user=word: ~{user}
    case "#" topic=word: ~{topic}
    case &"http://" url=Uri.uri_parser: {link: url}
    }
```

This parser consists of three cases:

- An @ character followed by a word, indicating a reference to the given user
- A # character followed by a word, indicating a reference to the given topic
- A link starting with the http:// string

This last case requires some additional explanation. We use a URI parser from the standard library, Uri.uri_parser. However, this parser is liberal as it accepts go.To as a valid URL. Indeed, as most users omit *http://* from URLs, go.To can be interpreted as a URL (and the domain exists), but it can also just be a missing whitespace in a sentence as in "We should go.To be there…". Therefore, we put an additional restriction that the URL should start with the http:// string.

This is where the new &exp construction comes in. It tries to parse using exp, and if that fails, the &exp expression fails too. However, if it succeeds, the parsing continues, but as though the parsing of exp consumed no input. In other words, this allows us to check whether exp would succeed at this point in the input, without really performing this parsing (in a sense). This operator is called a *logical predicate*. It allows us to perform a look-ahead in the parsed input. It has important implications for the expressive power of PEG, but this is a subject beyond the scope of this book.

We are now ready to write a parser for a *message segment*, which can be either one of the special elements mentioned earlier (user, topic, or link) or a piece of text:

```
segment_parser = parser {
    case ~element: element
    case text=word: {~text}
    case c=(.): {text: Text.to_string(c)}
    }
```

This parser has three cases:

- The first one takes care of special elements.
- The second one parses a word (as we defined it earlier) as text.
- The last one just consumes a single character.

Now a message simply consists of a number of such segments, and therefore, we can parse it with:

```
msg_parser = parser { case res=segment_parser*: res }
```

You may be wondering why we needed two separate cases for a word and a single character in the segment_parser. If we keep only the case for a single character, the message xxhttp://example.go would be parsed as text xx, followed by a link to *http://example.go*. This does not match our needs, and therefore, we parse one word at a time which, in this case, would result in the text xxhttp, followed by three special characters: ://. We still need the case for a single character to consume all characters that are not covered by the word case (punctuation marks and such).

Modeling Messages

We are now ready to provide a model for Birdy messages. We create a model file, *src/model/msg.opa*, and add it to the project (i.e., to the *opa.conf* file).

We then provide a definition for a message, Msg.t, which consists of the message content (content), its author (author), and the date it was published (created_at). We make it abstract as well:

```
abstract type Msg.t =
  { string content,
    User.t author,
    Date.date created_at
  }
```

We also introduce a type for a message segment, Msg.segment, in the sense introduced in the previous section:

```
type Msg.segment =
  { string text } or
  { Uri.uri link } or
  { User.name user } or
  { Topic.t topic }
```

Finally, we build a `Msg` module, with two accessory functions for message fields and a function to create a new message, as well as the parser we developed previously. We expose this parser as an `analyze` function, which takes a message, `Msg.t`, and returns the list of segments, `list(Msg.segment)`, it is composed of:

```
module Msg {

  function Msg.t create(User.t author, string content) {
    { ~content, ~author, created_at: Date.now() }
  }

  function get_author(Msg.t msg) { msg.author }
  function get_created_at(Msg.t msg) { msg.created_at }

  private function list(Msg.segment) analyze(Msg.t msg) {
    word = parser { case word=([a-zA-Z0-9_\-]+) -> Text.to_string(word) }
    element = parser {
    case "@" user=word: ~{user}
    case "#" topic=word: ~{topic}
    case &"http://" url=Uri.uri_parser: {link: url}
    }
    segment_parser = parser {
    case ~element: element
    case text=word: {~text}
    case c=(.): {text: Text.to_string(c)}
    }
    msg_parser = parser { case res=segment_parser*: res }
    Parser.parse(msg_parser, msg.content)
  }

}
```

Rendering Messages

It's time to turn our attention to the user interface. Let's create an *src/view/msg.opa* file; we'll use the same filename as before, as we are still dealing with messages, but we'll put it in the *view* directory. Also, the model code was placed in the `Msg` module, but all the code of this chapter will go into the `MsgUI` module. We'll then add it to the project as usual, in *src/opa.conf*.

We will first write a function to show (render) a message to the user:

```
function xhtml render(Msg.t msg) {
  msg_author = Msg.get_author(msg)
  <div class=well>
    <p class="author-info">
      <strong><a href="/user/{msg_author}">@{msg_author}</a></strong>
      <span>{Date.to_string(Msg.get_created_at(msg))}</span>
    </p>
    <p>
```

```
        {List.map(render_segment, Msg.analyze(msg))}
      </p>
    </div>
  }
```

This function creates a `<div>` with a `well` class, which is Bootstrap markup for a page element with an inset effect. The element consists of two paragraphs (`<p>`). The first one contains a `<strong>` tag (bold text) which contains a link to the author, `msg_author`, and a `<span>` tag which contains the message creation date. Note how we use accessor methods from the `Msg` module; this is because the `Msg.t` type is abstract, and hence, its structure is only visible in the `birdy.model` package and outside of it must be manipulated with functions from that package. This is *data abstraction* at work.

The second paragraph contains the text of the message itself. To obtain it, we use the `Msg.analyze` function which gets the list of the message segments, and then we use the `List.map` function to convert each segment into its HTML representation using the following `render_segment` function:

```
  private function render_segment(Msg.segment seg) {
    match (seg) {
    case ~{user}:
      <b><a class=ref-user href="/user/{user}">@{user}</a></b>
    case ~{topic}:
      <i><a class=ref-topic href="/topic/{topic}">#{topic}</a></i>
    case ~{link}:
      <a href={link}>{Uri.to_string(link)}</a>
    case ~{text}:
      <>{text}</>
    }
  }
```

This function just does the pattern matching of the segment type, and for every possible variant produces its HTML representation: both user mentions and topics are rendered as links, the former with a bold style (`<b>`) and linking to `/user/[USERNAME]` URLs and the latter with italics (`<i>`) and linking to `/topic/[TOPICNAME]`. We will talk about how we are going to handle those URLs in "User and Topic Pages" (page 142). Link segments are just rendered as HTML links (`<a>`) and `text` as normal text.

There is one small caveat. If you try to use the preceding code to render a message, you will be greeted with the following message:

```
Can't make an xml with {email : Email.email; username : string}
```

This is because in the earlier snippet, in the `render` function, we used an insert with a `User.t` value of the message author:

```
[...]
    <strong><a href="/user/{msg_author}">@{msg_author}</a></strong>
[...]
```

The error message essentially says that the Opa compiler does not know how to display values of that type. We can instruct it by creating an *xmlizer*, which is a special function that converts an arbitrary data type to HTML. For User.t values, it could look as follows:

```
@xmlizer(User.t) function user_to_xml(user) {
  <>{user.username}</>
}
```

The return type of this function must be of type xhtml. The only special thing about this function is the @xmlizer(User.t) annotation, which translates to "This is a function that converts User.t values into HTML."

There is an equivalent mechanism of *stringifiers* and an @stringifier(type) annotation, which are used for conversions to *strings*:

```
@stringifier(User.t) function user_to_string(user) {
  user.username
}
```

Let's add those two functions to our User module.

Reactive UI: Live Preview

We will now work on the feature that allows users to enter new messages. To make it more user-friendly, we will add a real-time preview that displays the formatted message while the user is typing.

Let's start by creating an interactive button that opens a modal window for entering a new message:

```
window_id = "msgbox"

function html() {
  match (User.get_logged_user()) {
  case {guest}: <></>
  case {user: _}:
    <a class="btn btn-primary pull-right" data-toggle=modal href="#{window_id}">
      <i class="icon-edit icon-white" />
      New message
    </a>
  }
}
```

The feature of adding new messages is only available to logged-in users who will see a Bootstrap button that opens the modal window identified by window_id [you learned how to deal with modal windows in "Bootstrap Widgets: Modal Windows" (page 88)]. For unlogged guests, we just return an empty snippet.

Now we will work on the modal window itself:

```
private preview_content_id = "preview_content"
private input_box_id = "input_box"

function modal_window_html() {
    match (User.get_logged_user()) {
    case {guest}: <></>
    case ~{user}:
      win_body =
        <textarea id={input_box_id} onready={update_preview(user)} onkeyup=
        {update_preview(user)} placeholder="Compose a message"/>
        <div id=#preview_container>
          <p class=badge>Preview</p>
          <div id={preview_content_id} />
        </div>
      win_footer =
        <>
          Post button will appear here
        </>
      Modal.make(window_id, <>What's on your mind?</>, win_body, win_footer, Mo-
dal.
      default_options)
    }
}
```

Again, we only create this for logged-in users. The modal body contains a `<textarea>`
with an `input_box_id` for the user's message and a `<div>` element with the `preview_con
tent_id` preview. Besides that, the input text area contains a placeholder and event
handlers for `onready` and `onkeyup` events, both invoking the `update_preview` function.
This means this function will be called when the window is created (`onready`) and every
time the user edits the message (`onkeyup`), and will update the live preview. In the modal
footer, for the moment, we add some temporary text for the forthcoming Post button.

Here is a very simple event handler, the `update_preview` function:

```
private client function update_preview(user)(_) {
  msg = Dom.get_value(#{input_box_id})
     |> Msg.create(user, _)
  #{preview_content_id} = render(msg)
}
```

In the preceding code, first we get the content of the text box with `Dom.get_value`, and
then we turn it into a message with the `Msg.create` function that we wrote previously.
In the last line of the function, we update the preview container (accessing it by its ID:
`preview_content_id`) with the rendered version of the message, obtained with our
`render` function.

All that remains to be done is to hook up our message creation button. For the best user experience we will make it accessible all the time, and therefore place it in the top bar of the app. To do so, we add a call to `MsgUI.html` in the `html` function in *src/view/topbar.opa*:

```
function html() {
  <a class=brand href="/">
    Birdy
  </a> <+>
  MsgUI.html() <+>
  user_menu()
}
```

It's better to place the modal window content outside of the top bar, to minimize the depth of the HTML structure. Therefore, we add some modal window HTML to the `page_template` function in *src/view/page.opa*:

```
function page_template(title, content) {
[...]
  <div id=#main>
    <span id=#notice class=container>{notice}</span>
    {content}
    {Signin.modal_window_html()}
    {Signup.modal_window_html()}
    {MsgUI.modal_window_html()}
  </div>
[...]
}
```

We're done! If you compile and run your Birdy application, after signing in you should see the "New message" button in the top bar similar to Figure 9-1.

Figure 9-1. Birdy "New message" button is displayed in the top-bar

Clicking on the "New message" button results in a modal window similar to the one shown in Figure 9-2.

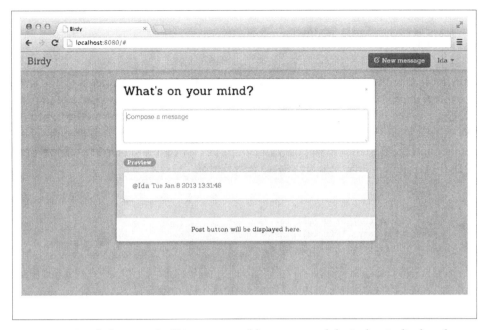

Figure 9-2. By clicking on the "New message" button a modal window is displayed

Let's make the following two improvements to this page:

- Add a message submission button to the modal window.
- Add an info box indicating how many characters have been entered. Let's stick to the micro-blogging tradition and limit messages to 140 characters in length.

In addition to this, the character counter will switch to a warning mode when the message size limit is approached, and to an error mode once the limit has been exceeded. In this last case, the submission button will also be disabled.

We'll start with a few constants for characters limits and UI element identifiers:

```
private MAX_MSG_LENGTH = 140
private MSG_WARN_LENGTH = 120

private chars_left_id = "chars_left"
private submit_btn_id = "submit_btn"
```

Getting the current message and closing the window are tasks that will now be performed in more than one place, so it is better to factor them out into dedicated functions:

```
private client function get_msg(user) {
  Dom.get_value(#{input_box_id})
  |> Msg.create(user, _)
}
```

```
private client function close() {
  Modal.hide(#{window_id})
}
```

Now let's place the character counter and Post button HTML elements to the win_
footer in the modal_window_html function. For a nicer display, we would like to place
the character counter on the left side of the footer, and the Post button on the right side.
We will use a parent <span> element with Bootstrap's pull-left class to float the character counter to the left. We will use Bootstrap's pull-right and btn btn-large btn-
primary classes for a nice, highly visible Post button:

```
[...]
win_footer =
  <span class="char-wrap pull-left">
    <span id={chars_left_id} class="char"/>
    characters left
  </span>
  <button id={submit_btn_id} disabled=disabled class="pull-right btn btn-large
btn-primary disabled" onclick={submit(user)}>
    Post
  </button>
[...]
```

Now we need the submit function that is invoked once the user decides to approve and
post his message:

```
private function submit(user)(_) {
  get_msg(user) |> Msg.store;
  Dom.clear_value(#{input_box_id});
  close();
  Client.reload();
}
```

In the four lines of this function we respectively are doing the following, in the order
shown:

1. Constructing the message and storing it by invoking Msg.store

2. Clearing the input box so that the creation of the next message will start with an
   empty box

3. Closing the modal window

4. Reloading the page to see the posted message

After we enter a message, it does not appear on the current page, even if it belongs there. One can see it only after refreshing the browser window. We solve this problem by always enforcing page refresh after publishing a new message. We'll return to this problem in Chapter 10.

The function that stores messages belongs to the Msg module in *src/model/msg.opa*. For the moment, we will write an empty temporary function that will be replaced with a real one when we discuss storage in Chapter 10.

```
function store(Msg.t msg) {
  void
}
```

The last remaining bit is to update the update_preview function:

```
private client function update_preview(user)(_) {
  msg = get_msg(user)
  #{preview_content_id} = render(msg)

  // show status
  msg_len = Msg.length(msg)
  #{chars_left_id} = MAX_MSG_LENGTH - msg_len
  remove = Dom.remove_class
  add = Dom.add_class
  remove(#{chars_left_id}, "char-error");
  remove(#{chars_left_id}, "char-warning");
  remove(#{submit_btn_id}, "disabled");
  Dom.set_enabled(#{submit_btn_id}, true);

  if (msg_len > MAX_MSG_LENGTH) {
    add(#{chars_left_id}, "char-error");
    add(#{submit_btn_id}, "disabled");
    Dom.set_enabled(#{submit_btn_id}, false);
  } else if (msg_len > MSG_WARN_LENGTH) {
    add(#{chars_left_id}, "char-warning");
  }
}
```

The first two lines in the preceding code just update the message preview using the get_msg function that we factorized. Then we check the message length, using the Msg.length function that we need to add to the message model:

```
function int length(Msg.t msg) {
  String.length(msg.content)
}
```

The `Dom.add_class` (resp. `Dom.remove_class`) is a function that adds (resp. removes) a certain style class to a given HTML element. DOM classes are a set in that each element can have several classes. A common mistake web developers make is to write code in JavaScript, such as:

```
if $('foo').class == bar
```

instead of:

```
if class_contains($('foo'), bar)"
```

Opa makes it harder to make this kind of mistake.

We then remove all the warning/error styling from the element indicating the number of characters left and set the Post button to the enabled state. If the message is over its length limit, we add a `char-error` class to the `counter` element and disable the Post button. If the message is only over the warning threshold, we just add a `char-warning` to the `counter` element.

We are done! In Figure 9-3, the character count number is in orange to warn that only 5 characters are left. In Figure 9-4, the character count number is in red to indicate that we passed 140 characters limit. Both figures show the final version of the modal window we created in this chapter.

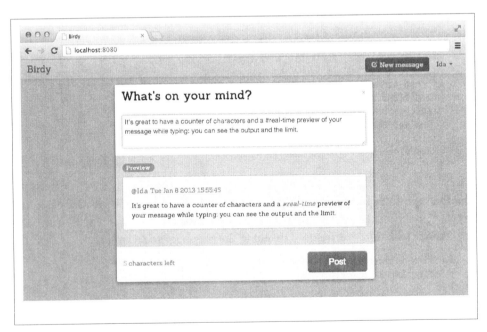

Figure 9-3. Birdy message preview with a warning

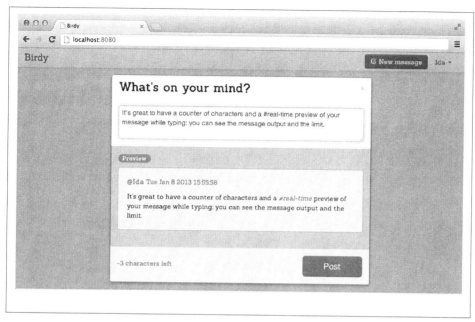

Figure 9-4. Birdy message preview with an error

Summary

In this chapter you learned how to:

- Use parsing for modeling
- Render messages
- Build a real-time preview

In Chapter 10 we will talk about data storage and retrieval. We will extend Birdy with real storage of new messages and with pages containing all messages for a given user or topic.

Data Storage and Querying: Storing and Fetching Relevant Messages

In this chapter you will learn more about data storage and retrieval (i.e., querying in Opa). We will start with some general concepts and then illustrate them by applying them to our Birdy app.

Collections in Opa: Lists, Sets, and Maps

Collections are used to represent multiple instances of the same type of data. In Opa, there are three primary types of collections:

- Lists
- Sets
- Maps

Lists represent a *sequence of items*. The order of items is the order of insertion. There may be multiple occurrences of the same value in a list. We talked about lists in "Recursive Types" (page 77).

Sets represent a group of items, ordered by an `order`, typically an alphanumerical sort. Sets cannot contain duplicates. They correspond to the mathematical notion of a set.

Maps are mappings from keys to values. They are often known by alternative names, such as *associative array* or *dictionary*. All the keys in a map are distinct.

Figure 10-1 depicts these different types of collections.

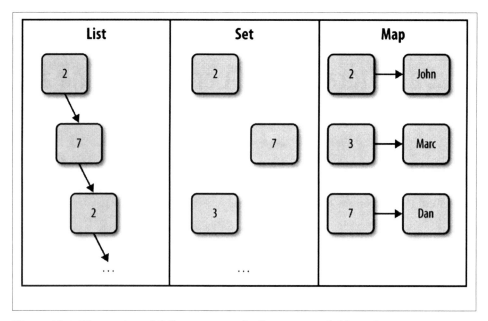

Figure 10-1. Illustration of different types of collections available in Opa

In the following sections we will discuss how to:

- Declare data for storage
- Write new or update previously stored data
- Query and retrieve data from storage

In each section we will also discuss features specific to records, lists, sets, and maps.

Declaring Data

We briefly talked about using databases in Opa in Chapter 4, but now it it time to present a more complete picture. Imagine that we want to write a movie-related application. Let's begin with a few relevant definitions.

 An *abstract type* is the directive that can be put on type definitions to hide the implementation of a type to the users of a library. Abstracting forces users to go through the interface of the library to build and manipulate values of that type.

Let's take the following type declaration:

```
abstract type Movie.id = int
type Movie.cert = {G} / {PG} / {PG-13} / {R} / {NC-17} / {X}

type Movie.crew =
  { Person.name director,
    list(Person.name) cast
  }
```

Movie.id is an abstract identifier of a movie; by keeping it abstract, we ensure that only the package in which this declaration occurs can manipulate such identifiers (e.g., create new values of that type). Movie.cert is an enumeration type for the U.S. motion picture rating system. Finally, Movie.crew holds (simplified) information about the people involved in the movie, with a single director and a list of the cast (in credits order).

We can now define a data type for a movie:

```
type Movie.t =
  { Movie.id id,
    string title,
    Movie.crew crew,
    int no_fans,
    int release_year,
    Movie.cert cert
  }
```

This movie consists of an ID, title, and crew (id, title, and crew), the number of fans (no_fans) of the movie, the year the movie was released (release_year), and the movie's rating (cert).

Now we are ready to declare the database:

```
database data {
  Movie.t /movies[{id}];
  map(Movie.id, string) /synopsis;
  int access_counter = 0;
}
```

The /data/synopsis path should look familiar [we briefly discussed maps in "Maps (Dictionaries)" (page 38)]; it declares a mapping from a Movie.id to its string synopsis.

As for /data/movies, it declares a *set* of values of type Movie.t. Here the set is indicated by the square brackets after the path. Within square brackets one needs to specify record fields (comma-separated) that will be used as the *primary key* for the set. This means the combination of those fields should be unique across all set values. In our simple example, we use a dedicated id field for that, which is a common strategy. Finally, we have a single int field, access_counter, which is initialized to 0.

Inserting/Updating Data

We already discussed some ways of adding/updating data in "Maps (Dictionaries)" (page 38). For example, adding a synopsis for the movie with ID 1 can be done with:[1]

```
/data/synopsis[1] <- "The aging patriarch of an organized crime dynasty
  transfers\
control of his clandestine empire to his reluctant son."
```

Can you guess which movie this synopsis belongs to?

Manipulating sets is done in a similar way:

```
/data/movies[{id: 1}] <-
  { id: 1,
    title: "The Godfather",
    crew:
      { director: "Francis Ford Coppola",
        cast: ["Marlon Brando", "Al Pacino", "James Caan"]
      },
    release_year: 1972,
    no_fans: 0,
    cert: {R}
  }
```

By providing only a subset of fields, we can do partial updates. The following examples also illustrate special features for updating `int` and `list` values:

```
// update a single field only
/data/movies[{id: 1}] <- { no_fans: 100 }
// increase no_fans by 1
/data/movies[{id: 1}] <- { no_fans++ }
// increase no_fans by 10
/data/movies[{id: 1}] <- { no_fans += 10 }

// add one element at the end of a list
/data/movies[{id: 1}]/crew/cast <+ "Richard S. Castellano"
// add several elements at the end of a list
/data/movies[{id: 1}]/crew/cast <++ ["Robert Duvall", "Sterling Hayden"]
// remove the first element of a list
/data/movies[{id: 1}]/crew/cast pop
// remove the last element of a list
/data/movies[{id: 1}]/crew/cast shift
```

Can you figure out what data about *The Godfather* is stored after all those operations? At the end of the complete program of this section, add the following:

```
println("{/data/movies[{id: 1}]}")
```

Then execute it and you will see something along the lines of this:

---

1. This synopsis was taken from the Internet Movie Database (IMDb), *http://imdb.com*.

```
{crew: {cast: [Al Pacino, Marlon Brando, Richard S. Castellano, Sterling
  Hayden],
  director: Francis Ford Coppola}, id: 1, no_fans: 111, release_year: 1972,
  title: The Godfather}
```

Reading (and Querying) Data

Now that you know how to declare and insert/update data, it's time to learn how to query the database to obtain required information. For simple structures, such as single values or records, all we can do is read the data; we discussed that many times already:

```
int n = /data/access_counter
```

However, things get more interesting with *collections*; that is, sets and maps. You already saw how to obtain single elements of collections, by *indexing* them:

```
movie_id = 1
string movie_synopsis = /data/synopsis[movie_id]
Movie.t movie_data = /data/movies[{id: movie_id}]
```

By indexing with a single value, which corresponds to the primary key for the set, we are certain to get no more than one value as a result. If the value does not exist, we will get a default result; if this is not what we need, we can always use the optional read operator:

```
option(string) opt_synopsis = ?/data/synopsis[movie_id]
option(Movie.t) opt_data = ?/data/movies[{id: movie_id}]
```

In this case, the result of the operation is none if the data does not exist, and some(...) if it does.

However, it is possible to use less precise indexing, in which case we may get more than one value as a result. The general scheme of such operations is the following:

```
/path/to/data[query; options]
```

Comparison operators represent an important building block of queries:

- == expr means the value equals that of expr.
- != expr means value does not equal that of expr.
- < expr, <= expr, > expr, and >= expr means the value is, respectively, less than, less than or equal to, greater than, or greater than or equal to that of expr.
- in expr means the value belongs to that of expr, where expr is a list.

Now a query can be any of the following:

op

> This is just a comparison operator; this query works for maps and means that we will be comparing keys of map entries.

`field op`
> This is the field's name followed by a comparison operator, meaning we filter entries based on comparisons of the record `field`.

`field/subfield op`
> This means we are using some field located deeper in the record structure for comparison.

`f1 op1, f2 op2, ...`
> This means we are using the comparison operator `op1` for field `f1`, `op2` for `f2`, and so on.

`field[_] op`
> The given field should contain a list, and this query means *any* element of the list passes the comparison.

There are also few binary operators to combine queries into more complex ones:

`q1 or q2`
> All values satisfying either query `q1` or query `q2`

`q1 and q2`
> All values satisfying both queries `q1` and `q2`

`not q`
> Values *not* satisfying the query q

Finally, the query options consist of a list of zero or more of the following entries, separated by semicolons:

`skip n`
> Skips the first n results (n should be an expression of type `int`).

`limit n`
> Limits the result to the maximum of n results (n should be an expression of type int).

`order fld1, fld2, ...`
> Specifies that the results should be ordered first by `fld1`, then `fld2`, and so on. Every `fld` value should be an identifier preceded by a plus sign (`+`) or a minus sign (`-`), with `+field` indicating ascending sorting by `field` and `-field` indicating descending sorting by `field`. It is also possible to use a version of `field=expr` to choose the order dynamically, where `expr` should be an expression evaluating to either {up} or {down}, indicating, respectively, ascending and descending order.

As mentioned earlier, such queries may result in more than one matching result; hence, the natural question is: what is the type of the result of such queries?

For maps, the type is the same as that of the queried map and the result of a query is a *sub-map*, that is, a map containing only part of the bindings of the original one.

For sets, the resultant value is of a special type, dbset(t, _), where t is the type of queried values and the second argument to the dbset type depends on what database backend is used; it can be safely ignored and replaced with an underscore in most cases.

The first step in dealing with such results will usually be to convert them to iterators with the DbSet.iterator function, and then to use standard functions from the Iter module.

As is often the case, an example is worth a thousand words, so let's look at a few examples of queries in action.

```
dbset(Movie.t, _) movies2000 = /data/movies[release_year == 2000]      ❶
Iter.t(Movie.t) it = DbSet.iterator(movies2000)                         ❷
xhtml movies = <>{Iter.map(Movie.render, it)}</>                        ❸

dbset(Movie.t, _) popular_movies = /data/movies[no_fans >= 1000]        ❹
dbset(Movie.t, _) children_movies = /data/movies[cert in [{G}, {PG}]]   ❺
dbset(Movie.t, _) new_popular = /data/movies[release_year >= 2000
  and no_fans >= 1000]                                                  ❻
dbset(Movie.t, _) non_x_rated = /data/movies[not cert == {X}]           ❼
dbset(Movie.t, _) some_popular = /data/movies[no_fans >= 10000;         ❽
  skip 100; limit 50; order -release_year, -no_fans]
dbset(Movie.t, _) by_coppola = /data/movies[
  crew/director == "Francis Ford Coppola"]                              ❾
dbset(Movie.t, _) with_pacino = /data/movies[
  crew/cast[_] == "Al Pacino"]                                          ❿

map(Movie.id, string) synops = /data/synopsis[>=1000 and <=1500]        ⓫
```

❶ Fetch all the movies that were released in the year 2000.

❷ Convert the results to an iterator.

❸ Use the Iter.map function to render all fetched movies with the Movie.render function and obtain the xhtml value.

❹ Fetch all movies with at least 1,000 fans.

❺ Fetch all movies with a G (General Audiences) or PG (Parental Guidance Suggested) age certificate.

❻ Fetch all movies released after 2000, that have at least 1,000 fans.

❼ Fetch all non-X-rated movies.

❽ Fetch the positions 101-150 (skip the first 100 and limit the results to 50) of movies with at least 10,000 fans, sorted by decreasing release year and, within the same release year, by the number of fans.

❾ Filter based on the subfield `director` of the `crew` record, effectively fetching all movies directed by Francis Ford Coppola.

❿ This is somewhat similar to the preceding query, but this time we filter based on a `cast` list of the `crew` record, fetching records where any elements of this list satisfy the given condition; this effectively fetches all movies starring Al Pacino.

⓫ Fetch a submap of the `/data/synopsis` map, for movies with an ID above 1,000 and below 1,500.

From these instructions and examples it is worth noting that sets and maps are very powerful for data storage. They essentially allow you to store collections of data, and then query them in fairly arbitrary ways. We will now discuss a powerful extension to the query mechanism: *projections*.

Projections

Imagine that we did not need all the information about some particular movie, but only the title of the movie with a particular ID. We could do that with the following query:

```
string title = /data/movies[{id: 1}]/title
```

The query `/data/movies[{id: 1}]` returns a single movie (with ID 1), and the remaining path, `/title`, means to project the resultant record to its single title field, which is of type `string`. Hence, that is the final type of such a query. It also works for queries with multiple results; for instance, to get the titles of all movies released in the year 2000, we could use the following query:

```
dbset(string, _) titles = /data/movies[release_year == 2000]/title
```

It is also possible to project into more than one field, although then, the syntax is slightly different. For example, imagine that we just wanted to fetch the title and the name of the director of a movie with a given ID; this query would do the job:

```
{string title, string director} m = /data/movies[{id: 1}].{title, crew.director}
```

Of course, it is also possible to do this kind of projection for multiple-result queries.

The main reason for using projections is *performance*. Most of the time it would be fine to fetch all the data from the database and only use the portions that we need. However, this may be an expensive operation, and we may be fetching a lot of information that we won't use anyway. Projections allow us to fine-tune the information transfered from the database to our program.

Data Manipulations in Birdy

You will now apply the knowledge you've gained from this chapter to Birdy. You will learn how to:

- Declare appropriate data storage
- Store new messages
- Retrieve messages based on some filtering criterion

Database Declaration

You've already manipulated Birdy messages and introduced a type representing them, `Msg.t`. Now it is time to save them in the database for persistent storage. First, we will recapitulate the definition of the `Msg.t` type introduced in "Modeling Messages" (page 117):

```
abstract type Msg.t =
  { string content,
    User.t author,
    Date.date created_at
  }
```

Since this is a self-contained type with all the information about the message, including its author, content, and creation date, one possibility is to store all the Birdy messages as a *set* of values of that type. This can be accomplished with the following database declaration:

```
database msgs {
  Msg.t /all[{author, created_at}]
}
```

Here, we declare a primary key consisting of two fields: the author and the creation date of the message. Since dates work with millisecond precision, we assume that no author will publish two different messages in the same millisecond, and hence, this is a unique primary key.

> If there is no natural primary key for the stored data, it is a frequent practice to introduce a dummy `id` field in the record, whose sole purpose is to identify the accompanying data and to serve as its primary key.

The previous database declaration relates to messages, so we could just add it to the */src/model/msg.opa* file. But as our strategy is to use a dedicated source file collecting all database declarations, we will slightly modify our declaration and add it to *src/model/data.opa*:

```
database birdy {
  User.info /users[{username}]
  Msg.t /msgs[{author, created_at}]
}
```

Storing New Messages

With the database declaration in place, we can now replace the dummy store function with a real one:

```
function void store(Msg.t msg) {
  /birdy/msgs[{author:msg.author, created_at:msg.created_at}] <- msg;
}
```

This function just adds a new entry to the /birdy/msgs set, indexed by the author and creation date of the given message.

 Running this program and monitoring message creation activity with a network profiler, which is an integral part of most modern browsers, reveals that creating a new message results in nine network requests.

This is because the store function uses the database, and hence resides on the server and needs to be accessed from the client when creating a new message. We can optimize this behavior by declaring this function as exposed:

```
exposed function void store(Msg.t msg) {
  /birdy/msgs[{author:msg.author, created_at:msg.cre-
ated_at}] <- msg;
}
```

After this change, the number of network requests drops to two: the expected single round-trip communication with the server.

Fetching Relevant Messages

While developing code to render messages in "Rendering Messages" (page 118) we introduced internal links of the shape /user/[USERNAME] and /topic/[TOPICNAME]. Those URLs will serve pages showing messages for a given user and topic, respectively. In order to develop such pages, we first need to fetch relevant messages that will be displayed on those pages; we will address this topic in this section and you will learn how to create those pages in "User and Topic Pages" (page 142).

What messages should be displayed on those pages? It is quite clear for the topics: every topic page should display all messages containing references to that topic. For the user pages, it is more complicated, as we want them to display:

- All messages posted by the page owner (i.e., the given user)
- Messages of all the users followed by the given user
- Messages concerning all the topics followed by the given user
- Messages mentioning the given user

First we'll turn our attention to a function that returns all the messages for a given topic. How do we write it? Recall that our type for a message looks as follows:

```
abstract type Msg.t =
  { string content,
    User.t author,
    Date.date created_at
  }
```

The content contains the content of the message as an unstructured string and we were using the analyze function to decompose it into segments, with user and topic references. However, with this data organization we have no chance of performing our task effectively, as we would need to fetch all the messages, analyze them one by one, and filter those that mention the topic we are interested in, an approach that would quickly become unacceptable in terms of performance.

How can we improve it? By employing the classic technique of enriching the data with redundant information that will enable us to perform the data querying we need effectively. In our case, we need to know which users and which topics every message refers to, so the solution is to add two new fields containing this information to our Msg.t type:

```
abstract type Msg.t =
  { string content,
    User.t author,
    Date.date created_at,
    list(Topic.t) topic_refs,
    list(User.name) user_refs
  }
```

We now need to initialize those two fields in the create function that creates a new message. We would like to reuse the analyze function to get the list of topics and users referenced in the message, but the problem is that this function takes a Msg.t argument and we cannot supply it yet, as at this point we are in the process of creating a new message value. The solution is to change the type of this function to operate on the string containing the raw content of the message, so this:

```
function list(Msg.segment) analyze(Msg.t msg) {
  ...
  Parser.parse(msg_parser, msg.content)
}
```

becomes this:

```
private function list(Msg.segment) analyze_content(string msg) {
  [...]
  Parser.parse(msg_parser, msg)
}

function list(Msg.segment) analyze(Msg.t msg) {
```

```
    analyze_content(msg.content)
  }
```

As you can see, we still make available the `analyze` function with the same type signature as before, which ensures that all the code outside of this module will work just as before. However, internally we develop a more low-level `analyze_content` function. We make it private to ensure that it is not visible from outside of the `Msg` module. We can now use it in the `create` function to initialize the `topic_refs` and `user_refs` fields:

```
function Msg.t create(User.t author, string content) {
  msg_segs = analyze_content(content)
  { ~content, ~author,
    created_at: Date.now(),
    topic_refs: get_all_topics(msg_segs),
    user_refs: get_all_users(msg_segs)
  }
}
```

We use two private functions, `get_all_topics` and `get_all_users`, that (given the list of segments of the message) return, respectively, the list of topics and users referenced in this message. A possible implementation of those functions could look as follows:

```
private function list(Topic.t) get_all_topics(list(Msg.segment) msg) {
  function filter_topics(seg) {
    match (seg) {
    case ~{topic}: some(topic)
    default: none
    }
  }
  List.filter_map(filter_topics, msg)
}

private function list(User.name) get_all_users(list(Msg.segment) msg) {
  function filter_users(seg) {
    match (seg) {
    case ~{user}: some(user)
    default: none
    }
  }
  List.filter_map(filter_users, msg)
}
```

Now we are done with user pages and topic fetching. It is easy to miss the importance of what happened here, though. Note that we changed the internal representation of messages in the system (by enriching it with some information) *without making any changes outside of the* `message` *module*. This was possible thanks to the fact that:

- Msg.t type was abstract, meaning the type could only be directly manipulated in the package in which it was declared and from the outside had to be accessed via the function provided in the package.
- We did not change the API (i.e., the signatures of the nonprivate functions) of the Msg module.

> This is an extremely important lesson in data encapsulation. Lessons that should be learned from this exercise are:
>
> - Whenever possible, make types abstract so that irrelevant implementation details are hidden in the given module.
> - Be careful when designing the public API of the module, which should only expose relevant features. Ideally, changing the internal representation of the type should be possible without making any changes to the public API, in which case such a change will only be local to the relevant package, just as was the case in our example.
>
> The bigger the team, the larger the project, and the more important it is to use abstract data types. For large projects, abstract data types might be one of the most powerful features of Opa.

Having our message type enriched with data, we can now easily write functions to return messages related (in the aforementioned sense) to a given topic or user:

```
function msgs_for_topic(Topic.t topic) {
    /birdy/msgs[topic_refs[_] == topic; order -created_at; limit 50]
}
```

To understand this better, let's take a look at all the components of this query and their meanings, step by step:

```
/msgs/all[                          ❶
    topic_refs[_] == topic;         ❷
    order -created_at;              ❸
    limit 50                        ❹
]
```

❶   Return all the messages...

❷   ... such that there is an element in the list topic_refs that is equal to topic.

❸   Sort the results by the creation date, in descending order (i.e., from newest to oldest).

❹   Limit the result to the first 50 entries (at most).

The function returning messages for a given user is only slightly more complicated:

```
function msgs_for_user(User.t user) {
  userdata = /birdy/users[{username: user.username}]      ❶
  /birdy/msgs[author.username in userdata.follows_users or ❷
          topic_refs[_] in userdata.follows_topics or      ❸
          user_refs[_] == user.username or                 ❹
          author.username == user.username;                ❺
          order -created_at;                               ❻
          limit 50]                                        ❼
}
```

❶ Fetch the data of the user with username user.username and bind it to userdata.

❷ Return all messages whose author belongs to the list userdata.follows_users, that is, to the list of those followed by the given user...

❸ ...or which refers to the topic that is on the list of topics followed by the given user (userdata.follows_topics)...

❹ ...or which refers to the given user...

❺ ...or whose author is the given user.

❻ Order the results in descending order by creation date.

❼ Limit the result to the first 50 entries (at most).

 In our example application we will always show, at most, the 50 most recent results. Usually, in a real application one would want to allow users to get access to older messages as well. This is typically achieved by *pagination* of results. To implement this, we would need to extend the preceding queries with a skip X; limit Y clause that would ensure that we obtain a window of, at most, Y results starting from position X.

User and Topic Pages

Now that we have functions to retrieve relevant messages, let's construct user and topic pages. First, we need to take care of the navigation, or URL dispatching. This is the role of the controller, so we will add two more cases to the Controller.dispatcher function in */src/controller/main.opa*:

```
function dispatcher(Uri.relative url) {
  match (url) {
  case {path: ["activation", activation_code] ...}:
    Signup.activate_user(activation_code)
  case {path:["user", user | _] ...}:
    Page.user_page(user)
  case {path:["topic", topic | _] ...}:
    Page.topic_page(topic)
  default:
```

```
    match (User.get_logged_user()) {
    case {~user}: Page.user_page(User.get_name(user))
    default: Page.main_page()
    }
  }
}
```

Note that we also modify `default`, adding a new `case` for the logged-in user that will display the user's page upon signing in when the URL doesn't change. This new `dispatcher` function needs to be connected to the Birdy `User` module, so we need to import `birdy.model` to the controller in the */src/opa.conf* file:

```
birdy.controller:
  import birdy.{model,view}
  [...]
```

We'll now turn our attention to the view in */src/view/page.opa*, as we need to add two functions used—`Page.topic_page` and `Page.user_page`—that will construct pages for a given topic and user, respectively. Those two pages are similar in the sense that they display a list of messages, so let's enclose this common feature in a function:

```
private function msgs_page(msgs, title, header) {
  msgs_iter = DbSet.iterator(msgs)
  msgs_html = Iter.map(MsgUI.render, msgs_iter)
  content =
    <div class=container>
      <div class=user-info>
        {header}
      </div>
      <div id=#msgs>
        {msgs_html}
      </div>
    </div>
  page_template(title, content, <></>)
}
```

Here, we've taken a list of database results as `msgs` and converted them to an iterator with `DbSet.iterator`. Then we converted those results to rendered messages using `Iter.map` with the `MsgUI.render` function. Finally, we built the HTML structure of our messages page to display messages.

With the messages page in place, we can easily build a page for a topic:

```
function topic_page(topic_name) {
  topic = Topic.create(topic_name)
  msgs = Msg.msgs_for_topic(topic)
  title = "#{topic}"
  header = <h3>{title}</h3>
  msgs_page(msgs, title, header)
}
```

Now we need a function to convert a string into a Topic.t type, which we place in the Topic module in */src/model/topic.opa*:

```
function Topic.t create(string topic) {
  topic
}
```

We create a page for a user in a similar way, but if the requested user does not exist, we will display an error page:

```
function user_page(username) {
  match (User.with_username(username)) {
  case {some: user}:
    msgs = Msg.msgs_for_user(user)
    title = "@{username}"
    header = <h3>{title}</h3>
    msgs_page(msgs, title, header)
  case {none}:
    page_template("Unknown user: {username}", <></>,
      alert("User {username} does not exist", "error")
    )
  }
}
```

We need to add a function to get a user with a given username to the User module:

```
function option(User.t) with_username(string name) {
  ?/birdy/users[{username: name}] |> Option.map(mk_view, _)
}
```

And that's it! By creating some messages and then clicking on the links contained in published messages or entering appropriate URLs by hand, you can verify that the pages work and display relevant messages.

Figure 10-2 is an example of a user page and Figure 10-3 is an example of a topic page.

Figure 10-2. Birdy user page

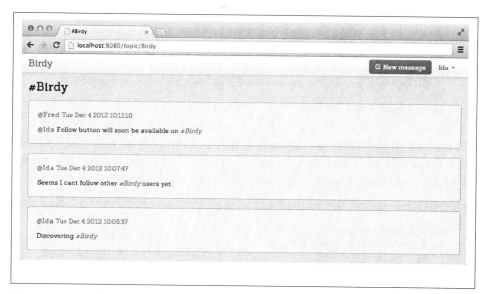

Figure 10-3. Birdy topic page

Following Users and Topics

Now we would like to add one more micro-blogging feature to our Birdy app: the ability to follow other users and topics. Our plan is to:

- Write functions to follow users.
- Write functions to follow topics.
- Build a Follow button and add it to the user interface.

The ability to follow will apply to logged-in users only, so first let's write a function in the User module that will allow us to perform some action with logged-in users:

```
private function do_if_logged_in(action) {
    match (get_logged_user()) {
      case {guest}: void
      case {user: me}: action(me)
    }
}
```

Following Users

Now let's use the preceding function to write a function to follow a user:

```
function follow_user(user) {
  function mk_follow(me) {
    /birdy/users[{username: me.username}]/follows_users <+ user.username
  }
  do_if_logged_in(mk_follow)
}
```

The function mk_follow allows us to update the list. As you saw in "Inserting/Updating Data" (page 132), <+ is used to add an element at the end of the list. We then use the do_if_logged_in function to apply it only to logged-in users.

Using the same method, let's write a function that allows us to unfollow a followed user:

```
function unfollow_user(user) {
  function mk_unfollow(me) {
    /birdy/users[username == me.username]/follows_users <-- [user.username]
  }
  do_if_logged_in(mk_unfollow)
}
```

Here we use <-- to remove the element from the list.

The next function we would like to write is a function that allows us to check if one given user A is followed by one logged-in user B:

```
function isFollowing_user(user) {
  match (get_logged_user()) {
  case {guest}: {unapplicable}
  case {user: me}:
    if (user.username == me.username) {
      {unapplicable}
    } else {
        if (/birdy/users[username == me.username and follows_users[_] ==
user.username]
          |> DbSet.iterator |> Iter.is_empty) {
        {not_following}
      } else {
        {following}
      }
    }
  }
}
```

This function applies to logged-in users and returns unapplicable for non-logged-in users as well as for the logged-in user B. The function looks for users who have the same username as logged-in user B and who follow given user A, and returns a DbSet that we transform to an iterator to check if the result is empty or not. If the result is empty, the function returns not_following; otherwise, it returns following.

Following Topics

Now we'll use the same methods we just used to write the follow_topic, unfollow_topic, and isFollowing_topic functions:

```
function follow_topic(topic) {
  function mk_follow(me) {
    /birdy/users[{username: me.username}]/follows_topics <+ topic
  }
  do_if_logged_in(mk_follow)
}

function unfollow_topic(topic) {
  function mk_unfollow(me) {
    /birdy/users[username == me.username]/follows_topics <-- [topic]
  }
  do_if_logged_in(mk_unfollow)
}

function isFollowing_topic(topic) {
  match (get_logged_user()) {
  case {guest}: {unapplicable}
  case {user: me}:
    if (/birdy/users[username == me.username and follows_topics[_] == topic]
        |> DbSet.iterator |> Iter.is_empty) {
      {not_following}
    } else {
```

```
            {following}
        }
    }
}
```

Follow Button

The last thing we need to address is the Follow button. Let's return to */src/view/page.opa* and modify our `msgs_page` function as follows:

```
private function msgs_page(msgs, title, header, follow, unfollow, isFollowing) {
  recursive function do_follow(_) {
    _ = follow();
    #follow_btn = follow_btn();
  }
  and function do_unfollow(_) {
    _ = unfollow();
    #follow_btn = follow_btn();
  }
  and function follow_btn() {
    match (isFollowing()) {
    case {unapplicable}: <></>
    case {following}: <a class="btn" onclick={do_unfollow}>Unfollow</a>
      case {not_following}: <a class="btn btn-primary" onclick={do_follow}><i
class="icon icon-white icon-plus"/> Follow</a>
    }
  }
  msgs_iter = DbSet.iterator(msgs)
  msgs_html = Iter.map(MsgUI.render, msgs_iter)
  content =
    <div class=container>
      <div class=user-info>
        {header}
        <div id=#follow_btn>{follow_btn()}</div>
      </div>
      {if (isFollowing() == {unapplicable} && Iter.is_empty(msgs_iter)) {
        <div class="well">
                <p>You don't have any messages yet. <a data-toggle=modal
href="#{MsgUI.window_id}">Compose a new message</a>.</p>
        </div>
      } else <></>}
      <div id=#msgs>
        {msgs_html}
      </div>
    </div>
  page_template(title, content, <></>)
}
```

We add the do_follow and do_unfollow functions that take the user or topic and reconstruct the Follow button, and then we write the follow_btn function that takes the state returned by isFollowing and returns the corresponding HTML. We use Bootstrap classes to distinguish the Follow and Unfollow buttons by color. We create a <div> element with a #follow_btn identifier and call the follow_btn function. For a better user experience, we create a special page for the user (first-time) who doesn't have any messages. We display a short notification about it and suggest that he create a new message. If the user has messages, they are displayed on the page.

Now let's call the follow, unfollow, and isFollowing functions in the topic_page and user_page functions:

```
function topic_page(topic_name) {
  topic = Topic.create(topic_name)
  msgs = Msg.msgs_for_topic(topic)
  title = "#{topic}"
  header = <h3>{title}</h3>
  function follow() { User.follow_topic(topic) }
  function unfollow() { User.unfollow_topic(topic) }
  function isFollowing() { User.isFollowing_topic(topic) }
  msgs_page(msgs, title, header, follow, unfollow, isFollowing)
}

function user_page(username) {
  match (User.with_username(username)) {
  case {some: user}:
    msgs = Msg.msgs_for_user(user)
    title = "@{username}"
    header = <h3>{title}</h3>
    function follow() { User.follow_user(user) }
    function unfollow() { User.unfollow_user(user) }
    function isFollowing() { User.isFollowing_user(user) }
    msgs_page(msgs, title, header, follow, unfollow, isFollowing)
  case {none}:
    page_template("Unknown user: {username}", <></>,
      alert("User {username} does not exist", "error")
    )
  }
}
```

Compile and run your Birdy application to check the Follow button. Figure 10-4 shows a user's page viewed by another logged-in user who doesn't follow him. Figure 10-5 shows the topic page that is followed by the logged-in user: the Follow button has turned into an Unfollow button.

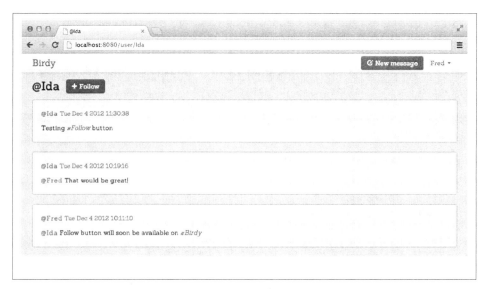

Figure 10-4. Following a Birdy user

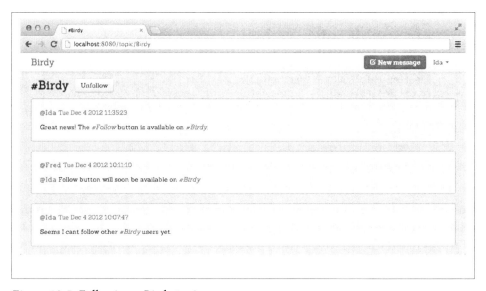

Figure 10-5. Following a Birdy topic

This concludes our detailed tour of the functions we have implemented in Birdy. Now it's time to play.

Exercise

Remember when we talked about enforcing page refresh to display a user's new messages in "Rendering Messages" (page 118)? We solved half of the problem. However, what if some other user entered a message that should be displayed on the current page? In such a case, Twitter displays a window saying that there are *N new messages* and by clicking on it one can see them.

Apply what you learned when writing the chat application in Chapter 6 to display all relevant messages in real time in Birdy.

Summary

In this chapter you learned about data storage and querying. Specifically, you learned how to:

- Declare, insert, update, read, and acquire data
- Store and fetch relevant messages
- Handle navigation
- Build functions to follow and unfollow users

We hope that by reading this book you have learned many things about Opa and web programming. Programming is a never-ending subject, and our goal was to give you enough knowledge to fly on your own and build great applications or even companies.

As a last reminder, there are many online resources to help you in your quest to build great applications in Opa, including the following:

- The Opa forum, available at *http://forum.opalang.org*, is a great start.
- The online documentation at *http://doc.opalang.org* is the best way to browse the standard library.
- The GitHub repository at *http://github.com/MLstate/opalang* hosts a wiki and provides a way to report issues.

That's all, folks!

About the Authors

Henri Binsztok is the creator of Opa and was previously a researcher and teacher at the University of Paris.

Adam Koprowski is a software developer at Google. He has authored numerous articles on Opa. Adam was previously a researcher at Radboud University.

Ida Swarczewskaja graduated from Tallinn University of Technology. She is leading the work on the user experience and design of the Opa portal, tools, demos, and applications.

Colophon

The animal on the cover of *Opa: Up and Running* is the Opah fish (*Lampris guttatus*).

The cover image is from Johnson's *Natural History*. The cover font is Adobe ITC Garamond. The text font is Adobe Minion Pro; the heading font is Adobe Myriad Condensed; and the code font is Dalton Maag's Ubuntu Mono.

Get even more for your money.

Join the O'Reilly Community, and register the O'Reilly books you own. It's free, and you'll get:

- $4.99 ebook upgrade offer
- 40% upgrade offer on O'Reilly print books
- Membership discounts on books and events
- Free lifetime updates to ebooks and videos
- Multiple ebook formats, DRM FREE
- Participation in the O'Reilly community
- Newsletters
- Account management
- 100% Satisfaction Guarantee

Signing up is easy:

1. **Go to: oreilly.com/go/register**
2. **Create an O'Reilly login.**
3. **Provide your address.**
4. **Register your books.**

Note: English-language books only

To order books online:
oreilly.com/store

For questions about products or an order:
orders@oreilly.com

To sign up to get topic-specific email announcements and/or news about upcoming books, conferences, special offers, and new technologies:
elists@oreilly.com

For technical questions about book content:
booktech@oreilly.com

To submit new book proposals to our editors:
proposals@oreilly.com

O'Reilly books are available in multiple DRM-free ebook formats. For more information:
oreilly.com/ebooks

Spreading the knowledge of innovators | oreilly.com

Lightning Source UK Ltd.
Milton Keynes UK
UKOW021548270313

208273UK00004B/27/P